# DECADES

T0268078

# QUEEN
## in the 1970s

James Griffiths

SONICBOND

sonicbondpublishing.com

Sonicbond Publishing Limited
www.sonicbondpublishing.co.uk
Email: info@sonicbondpublishing.co.uk

First Published in the United Kingdom 2023
First Published in the United States 2023

British Library Cataloguing in Publication Data:
A Catalogue record for this book is available from the British Library

Copyright Andrew James Griffiths 2023

ISBN 978-1-78952-265-5

Typeset in ITC Garamond Std & ITC Avant Garde Gothic Pro
Printed and bound in England
Graphic design and typesetting: Full Moon Media

# DECADES

# QUEEN
## in the 1970s

James Griffiths

sonicbondpublishing.com

**Follow us on social media:**
Twitter: https://twitter.com/SonicbondP
Instagram: https://www.instagram.com/sonicbondpublishing_/
Facebook: https://www.facebook.com/SonicbondPublishing/

Linktree QR code:

## Dedication

For Mum, Dad, Karen, Oliver & Rowan, with Love

# DECADES | Queen in the 1970s

## Contents

# Introduction and acknowledgements

It's a curious irony that just as I finished writing this book in 2022, Queen Elizabeth II passed away. Freddie Mercury had of course loved the Queen and everything about the royal family. While his band was scuffling around in the early-1970s, he avidly perused the pages of magazines devoted to chronicling the fabulous opulence of the Windsors. It was the era of glam rock, but Mercury's conception of glamour had a regal flavour. It was this ingenious twist that lent Queen a visual style and musical signature that was uniquely their own.

Of course, Freddie wasn't just influenced by the grandiloquence of the royals – in his mind, their exotic image was all-of-a-piece with the theatrical flamboyance of Broadway musicals (He worshipped *Cabaret* star Liza Minnelli nearly as much as he did the Queen) and the androgynous allure of the new breed of pop star as personified by Marc Bolan and David Bowie. But when the chips were down, no one could out-pomp Her Royal Highness, and by any yardstick, she and her family were the ultimate show in town. Freddie knew that, but he still wanted to imitate and possibly compete with them.

With rock 'n' roll having traditionally been the music of teenage rebellion, Mercury's obsession with queenly grandeur was never going to go down well with critics. It also put off a fair few music fans. His royal ardour could manifest in various provocative ways – from swearing at journalists who refused to stand during the national anthem (which happened during at least one press launch), to insisting that a share of the band's 1977 tour earnings be siphoned off to help the Silver Jubilee fund. Late in the group's career, he even paraded about in a huge gown and crown at the end of their colossal stadium shows, to the accompaniment of the national anthem played on loud electric guitars. It was all done with a mischievous twinkle in his eye – something the band's detractors never quite seemed to grasp, but which the fans understood only too well.

I've been a Queen fan since 1977 (coincidentally, the year of the Silver Jubilee), having become an instant convert after seeing Freddie camping it up in a leotard in the 'We Are The Champions' video. I wasn't a habitual fan of men in leotards, but Freddie wore it well and sang with the voice of a rock-'n'-roll angel. The music behind him was majestic, bludgeoning and ever so slightly alarming. I was six years old and mesmerised, even more so when I saw the huge killer robot on the cover of their latest album *News of the World*. I got that terrifying-looking record for my seventh birthday, and the moment I heard track three, 'Sheer Heart Attack', I knew I'd found something that connected with me on a very profound level. 'Hey hey hey hey, it was the DNA'.

Shortly afterwards, their album *Live Killers* gave me my first experience of live rock music, after which my archaeology project began in earnest. Digging through record shops, I turned up Queen albums from yesteryear. I drooled over them and dreamed about owning them. Fortunately, I had very kind parents, so pretty much all of these records (over a period of two or three years) ended up coming home with me. Sitting in my bedroom, staring at the cover of *Sheer Heart Attack* and obsessing over why Roger Taylor was lolling upside down on the cover, I fantasized about being in Queen. I knew that was unlikely to ever happen, so I started dreaming that I was at least friends with the band. I remember listening to *The Game* in the summer of 1980 and pretending that Freddie and the guys were due to arrive at the house for a cup of tea and a slice of cake at any moment. I imagined them sitting in the living room, chatting to my parents and telling them about their plans for the next album and tour. I imagined going downstairs and asking Brian and Roger if they fancied coming outside for a game of swingball.

To me, Queen was more than just a band. They were my friends, my guides, and my teachers. I learned so much from them, priceless knowledge in the form of chord progressions, melodies, lyrics, and weird and wonderful sounds I couldn't begin to fathom. In their own sweet way as quirky populists and musical magpies, they taught me about opera, heavy rock, torch songs, gospel, ragtime, vaudeville, prog, blues, Dixieland jazz, soul, funk and 1950s rock 'n' roll. They also taught me about the importance of self-belief, the joys of overt theatricality and the sheer power of tireless creativity. They gave me a window into another world – a fantasy realm that was nothing like the humdrum realities of home life and school, but which also seemed oddly familiar to me. Quite simply, Freddie and Queen took my breath away.

Years later, when I was playing drums in my own group, my friend and bandmate Phil Cheshire and I obsessively watched the VHS tape *Queen Live at Wembley*, knocking back the beers and praying to whatever gods existed that one day we would come to know such glory. Auditioning bass players, we laid down a rule that anyone coming into our band *had* to like Queen. We just couldn't imagine playing with or even befriending anyone who didn't. As a drummer, I worked tirelessly at becoming as impressive as Roger Taylor, but never got anywhere near his dazzling flamboyance (I just hadn't listened to enough Surfaris records and didn't have the tigerskin pants). In the end, I gave up trying to be Roger, and became a music writer instead.

The first book I ever read about Queen was *These Are the Days of Our Lives* by Stephen Rider (1993). Sitting in a rain-lashed caravan on the west coast of Wales, I learned about the group's early years and marvelled at just how long they'd spent in the rock-'n'-roll wilderness before their lucky numbers came up. Since then, I've read many other Queen tomes and enjoyed them all (see the bibliography), so when Stephen Lambe at Sonicbond offered me the chance to tell my own version of the tale, I leapt at it. Coming to an already well-explored story like Queen's, I knew I had to somehow find my own spin on it, however modest. In the end, I opted simply to try and place the band in the context of their times (a prerequisite of all the books in the Decades series), and also to emphasise the four musicians' absolute commitment to each other, and their dogged pursuit of success. That's not to say they didn't have their problems, of course. But there never seemed to be any issue that they couldn't deal with. Whether it was Freddie's debauched lifestyle, Brian's perennial anxiety and depression, or simply Roger locking himself in a cupboard until he got his own way, they always managed to rise above whatever was going on. Only Freddie's death managed to stop them (temporarily), but this book doesn't follow the story as far as that.

I'd like to thank all the previous writers who have told this hugely-entertaining story, with two deserving special admiration. Firstly, plaudits go to Georg Purvis, whose immense *Queen: The Complete Works* is a goldmine of information. A terrific book I used in parallel was Benoît Clerc's *Queen: All the Songs*: a monumental hardback which I don't recommend dropping on your foot. Others can be found in this book's bibliography.

Thanks go to my unofficial fact and stat checker Richard McCook who helped me with my previous book *Squeeze: The Pop Music Played*, and who was again on-hand to scrutinise the endless release dates and chart positions. I'd also like to thank Bob Wegner for all the hard work he's put into his website *Queenlive.ca,* which was my regular resource for concert information. Bob's site is also a treasure trove of photos, which kept me distracted for many hours when I was supposed to be working.

Finally, the two biggest thank-yous are reserved for Stephen Lambe – for allowing me to join the legions of authors who have grappled with the Queen story – and the fine writer John Van der Kiste, who first put me in touch with Stephen and suggested I pitch him a few ideas. I owed you already John, and now I owe you more.

Apart from the obvious royal trappings, Queen Elizabeth II and Queen the rock band share one other quality: that of apparently always having been there. Try to imagine a world without 'Bohemian Rhapsody', and you'll see what I mean. In truth, that was only a song that fell off a reel of much-abused tape one day in the middle of the 1970s. The story of what Queen did on that day, and many other such days between 1970 and 1979, is the subject and story of this book. I hope you enjoy it.

# A Word on the Text

Where possible, I've tried to list the relevant album credits as they appeared in the original album liner notes. This has particular relevance when it comes to stating which instruments the various musicians played on the records. Queen often swapped instruments or introduced novel new instruments into their music. Where this happened, I allowed myself the luxury of describing it in the main narrative rather than attempting to list everything in the album credits.

# Prelude: Paradise Lost

The spice-rich Tanzanian archipelago of Zanzibar reclines in the Indian Ocean just off the coast of East Africa. A sun-drenched land of sultan's palaces, ancient Arabian forts and bustling bazaars, it's also the birthplace of a man who helped shape the history of British rock music.

On Thursday, 5 September 1946, a child was born at Zanzibar's Government Hospital, to an Indian couple of Persian descent. His parents called him Farrokh, rejoicing as they did so (knowing nothing of his mercurial future) that now having had a son, their family name Bulsara would continue into the next generation. Farrokh's parents Bomi and Jer were originally from Mumbai: then known as Bombay. His father had moved to the British-controlled Zanzibar several years before in search of work, eventually ending up as a government cashier. After returning to Bombay to marry Jer, he brought her back to the island, and the couple settled down to raise a family. Six years after Farrokh came a daughter they named Kashmira.

Bomi and Jer were Parsees – their Persian ancestry required them to follow the monotheistic Iranian religion of Zoroastrianism. Theirs was a strict and socially-conservative belief system – among its many precepts, the idea that homosexuality was a crime against God. Despite this, the Bulsaras managed to not be too austere as parents. Farrokh and his younger sister enjoyed a life of considerable comfort, with domestic servants at their beck and call.

Farrokh grew up to be a precocious child, fond of painting, drawing and music. Despite this, he was almost painfully shy – his cousin Perviz later remembering him as barely able to utter a word whenever he came to stay with her parents in India during the school holidays. Farrokh was transported by the idyllic beauty of his physical surroundings. In later years he wrote fantasy and fairy-tale-themed songs such as 'Seven Seas Of Rhye' and 'My Fairy King', insisting they were purely fictional. Yet it's difficult to believe such rock-'n'-roll fantasias weren't at least subconsciously inspired by the exotic landscapes of Zanzibar and India.

Though the Bulsaras were loving parents in their way, they thought nothing of packing Farrokh off to a private boarding school in Panchgani, Western India, when he was just eight years old. St Peter's offered a full English education and keenly promoted sports and the arts. But Farrokh's early years at the school were marred by acute homesickness and a creeping sense that his parents had abandoned him. Despite this, he excelled in athletics, art, drama and music. He studied classical piano, joined the choir and developed a passion for opera. He also acquired the name Freddie – courtesy of his friends and teachers, who struggled with the pronunciation of Farrokh. A rather-less-flattering nickname (used by his girlfriend Gita when Farrokh was 14) was Bucky – a reference to his oversized teeth, which protruded endearingly and made him self-conscious.

Freddie also fell in love with rock 'n' roll, courtesy of Radio Ceylon blasting a steady diet of Elvis, Little Richard and Fats Domino. Smitten by Fats' rolling New Orleans ivory-tickling, Freddie began to bash out improvised boogie-woogie pieces on the school piano, eventually joining his first band, The Hectics, who played various functions, and by all accounts, got the girls screaming. Embarrassed about his Bugs Bunny teeth, Freddie allowed himself to melt into the background and play the piano while his friend Bruce Murray fronted the group. Eventually, Freddie's schoolwork suffered as he lost interest in academia and realised that his true talents lay elsewhere.

He ended up leaving school without any O-levels and returned to Zanzibar to complete his education at the Roman Catholic St Joseph's Convent school. He emerged from his childhood as a shy, private young man with a tendency towards vanity. In later years – perhaps remembering his parents' emotional distance – he described himself as having an incredibly soft centre protected by an indestructible, hard outer shell. A craving for love and affection of all kinds stayed with him for the rest of his life.

Whether or not Freddie felt his island home was paradise, he was destined to be torn away from it before he was 20. In 1964, the Zanzibar Revolution led to the African revolutionaries' overthrowing of the Arab sultan. With bloody battles being fought in the street, the terrified Bulsaras fled for their lives and headed for England – a logical destination, given that Freddie's father had worked for the British regime in Zanzibar.

The family moved into a modest house at 22 Gladstone Avenue, Feltham, in the London borough of Hounslow. Bomi found work as a cashier for the Forte catering group, and his wife took a job in a local supermarket. Freddie applied for shift work on a nearby trading estate where, on the receiving end of taunts about his feminine hands, he claimed to be an artist biding his time before the inevitable big break.

Though acclimatising to the damp English weather initially left Freddie out of sorts, he soon found that being transplanted onto British soil in 1964 – the year that Beatlemania exploded – was a blessing in disguise. Before long, the ground beneath his feet seemed to be cracking open with possibilities.

A cousin from his childhood days in Zanzibar later spoke of Freddie's desire to sever all links with his geographical and ethnic past, particularly as Zoroastrianism was a faith deeply hostile to homosexuality. (Freddie's complex and ambiguous sexuality had not yet fully manifested.) Eventually, he was even to discard his family surname, take on a whole new identity and become one of the biggest music stars of the 20th century. But before any of that could happen, there were three specific people he needed to meet.

# 1968/1969 - A Sudden Passion for Dentistry

When the 19-year-old Roger Meddows Taylor announced in the summer of 1968 that he'd decided to enrol on a dentistry course, there was some surprise within his peer group and the wider community of Truro in South-West England. It wasn't that anyone doubted that the Norfolk-born Roger had the brains to become a dentist – unlike many British wannabe rock stars of his era, he'd prospered at school (though he didn't enjoy studying), and there was no doubt he'd pursue a skilled profession of some kind. But until that summer, he'd never – to anyone's knowledge – expressed the slightest interest in dentistry. A 1985 edition of Roger's old school magazine revealed that his miraculous conversion to dentistry was triggered by the deputy head Dick Taylor, who'd advised him that there wasn't much of a financial future in playing the drums. In fact, drumming was just one string to Roger's bow – he'd started out playing the ukulele, then moved to guitar.

But drums became the fair-haired, blue-eyed Roger's overriding love. Inspired by the early records of Little Richard and Jerry Lee Lewis, he was spurred into action by the arrival of the skiffle craze in the early-1960s. He wasted no time asking his dad for a drum kit, and soon began banging about in his parents' garage. In 1963 he heard 'Wipe Out' – a seminal slice of percussive glory by the American instrumental band The Surfaris. The driving toms played by drummer Ron Wilson sent Roger's head into a spin. Along with Sandy Nelson's 'Let There Be Drums', 'Wipe Out' proved to be a pivotal influence.

Roger started gigging around Truro in a succession of bands, eventually becoming the drummer and lead vocalist of The Reaction, who are remembered as the town's most legendary musical attraction. They won multiple talent contests, and even supported The Kinks at the Flamingo Ballroom: one of the area's most prestigious venues. Not only had Roger carved a niche for himself as the most creative drummer in Cornwall, but his sparkling good looks also made him a local heartthrob. Rock-'n'-roll greatness surely beckoned.

Given that his sudden passion for studying dentistry involved transplanting himself to London – a city crowded with ambitious young musicians, managers, venues, recording studios and record labels – a suspicious soul might well conclude that Roger's plan to move had an ulterior motive. His mother thought so, telling her son that when he got to London, he wasn't to immediately start scouting around for like-minded, long-haired rock musicians to form a band with. Unfortunately for Mrs. Taylor, Roger was doing precisely that. Before the ink had dried on his London Hospital Medical College enrolment form, he'd begun auditioning for various bands, later remembering the unpleasant rigmarole of waiting in turn with '80 drum kits all in a row'. Eventually, courtesy of a note pinned up in the students' union at Imperial College, he hooked up with Tim Staffell – a bassist/singer studying at Ealing Art College – and Brian May: an alarmingly tall, thin, pale Physics graduate who'd started a PhD on the nature of zodiacal light. When Brian wasn't beavering away with his research, he was spending most of his time with Tim, rattling the walls with a rather unusual homemade electric guitar.

Having left his drum kit in Cornwall, Roger attended his initial Smile audition armed only with a humble set of bongos. He still managed to impress Brian and Tim enough for a second session to be arranged, this time in a jazz practice room at Imperial College, with a full drum set in attendance. It was there that Brian and Tim were blown away by Roger's Surfaris-inspired flamboyance, and by his ability to tune a snare drum. Brian later recalled that he and Tim thought Roger was the best drummer they'd ever seen. He was also a strong singer, whose high, keening falsetto – perfected during a boyhood stint in the Truro Cathedral Choir – was underpinned by a Rod Stewart-like gruffness. Roger was also impressed with Brian. Not only did they share an evangelical passion for the music of Jimi Hendrix, but Brian was also a devoted fan of Irish guitarist Rory Gallagher. He was even playing with Rory's exact setup of a Vox AC30 amplifier with a Dallas Rangemaster treble-booster unit. This clearly was a man who meant business. From the word go, it was evident there was a unique musical chemistry between Roger and Brian. The combination of Roger's thunderous drumming and the jumbo-jet roar of Brian's Red Special guitar sounded like a clarion call.

Meanwhile, Tim was a fine singer with an impressive vocal range, and was also a not-too-shabby harmonica player. The addition of music student Chris Smith on bluesy keyboards rounded out the lineup.

As Roger soon discovered, Smile wasn't the first band Brian and Tim had played in together. Their previous outfit had been 1984 – a group formed while both were pupils at Hampton Grammar School. They'd enjoyed the honour of supporting Jimi Hendrix, Traffic, Pink Floyd and Tyrannosaurus Rex at a 1967 Christmas charity concert at the Olympia Exhibition Centre. Despite this impressive credential, 1984 never progressed beyond amateur status, and fell apart shortly before Roger's arrival in London. However, Brian and Tim hadn't given up hopes of rock stardom.

For Brian Harold May, playing music was ostensibly a hobby to be enjoyed in the downtime between academic lectures. He'd grown up a studious only child whose father was an electronics engineer working as a senior draughtsman for the Ministry of Aviation. Though Harold May had encouraged his son's musical gifts by teaching him the ukulele, he also passed on his love for photography. Harold gave Brian a camera for his birthday, and later, when Brian showed an interest in astronomy, helped him build a telescope. By the time Brian began attending Hampton Grammar in 1958, he was already talking about becoming a professional astronomer. But the music bug had also bitten him, and he found himself obsessed with playing guitar.

Though he started off enjoying the strummed acoustic guitars of The Everly Brothers, Brian's true eureka moment came courtesy of American singer Rick Nelson's rockabilly guitarist James Burton. In a 2021 interview with Rick Beato on the latter's YouTube channel, Brian revealed, 'I wanted to do what Burton did on the 'Hello Mary Lou' solo. When he started doing that string-bending, I realised that the guitar wasn't just a backing instrument anymore'.

Brian loved the dexterity of players like Charlie Byrd, Django Reinhardt, Julian Bream and Andrés Segovia, but he was also drawn to guitarists who used technology to enhance their sound. Brian told Beato: 'I liked the multitracked things that Chet Atkins did, and then I got hold of a couple of records by Les Paul, who was doing stuff with sped-up tapes'.

As someone attracted to music and science, it isn't surprising that Brian's passion for guitar accompanied an urge to push technological boundaries. His first and grandest experiment had been building his own guitar. Wanting a Fender Stratocaster but not being able to afford one, he'd hit on the idea of making his own custom instrument. He enlisted his dad's help to construct a unique instrument from bits and pieces, including the top of an oak table (the guitar's body), a mahogany fireplace (the neck), and a knitting needle (the vibrato arm) belonging to his mother. The guitar had unique design specifications – not the least of which was a set of phased pickup controls which created unearthly shrieking tones which couldn't be found on any shop-bought instrument. As his *pièce de résistance*, Brian elected to play his guitar with a sixpence instead of a plectrum, which lent an abrasive quality to the sound.

Even more than in 1984, Brian's Red Special helped to define Smile's heavy progressive sound. Another dimension was now added by Roger's powerful drumming and strong melodic backing vocals. By autumn 1968, Smile had secured their first major gig: supporting Pink Floyd at Imperial College on 26 October. Before long, they became the *de facto* house band at Imperial, with a growing following and repertoire of original material. The stage seemed set for a professional career. But, as it turned out, one specific ingredient was missing.

According to Freddie Bulsara, what Smile lacked was a sense of showmanship. A friend of Chris and Tim's, Freddie was a charismatic graphic-art student from Ealing College. He'd been on the scene for some time, having been an unofficial roadie for 1984 in their final months. Tim first brought Freddie along to a Smile rehearsal in early 1969, but it was only after Freddie saw them play live that he began berating them for their lack of visual appeal. In his view, a band shouldn't just saunter onstage in their street clothes and play without looking at the audience – a common sight now that rock musicians had begun distancing themselves from the *show-biz* requirements of chart-bound pop music. Freddie said they should instead put on a grand show, project a dark, mysterious image, and perhaps even toy with a little androgynous glamour.

Though Freddie hadn't written any songs yet, he claimed to know better than Smile how *their* songs should be arranged. Brian and Roger liked him, laughing whenever he began expounding his ideas – usually delivered with a lot of arm-waving the moment the band came off stage.

Freddie soon fell in love with Smile's music, often hopping into their van for journeys down to Truro, where Roger's hometown connections ensured there was a ready-made circuit of decent venues to play at. Freddie had musical ambitions of his own but had yet to try making his mark on the live London scene. Quizzing Freddie about his background, Roger and Brian found him reluctant to discuss his past in any detail. But he happily explained that he'd always loved music and art. After arriving in England with his family a few years before, he'd obtained an A-level from Isleworth Polytechnic (where he'd also acted in plays and tried to form a band) in order to enrol on a fashion course at Ealing College. Later, he transferred to the diploma in graphic design and illustration. This, he reasoned, at least fed into his love of all things visual.

Freddie proved to be an average student, hurrying through assignments so he could get back to his favourite activity of plonking around on the college piano. He was totally consumed with music and the idea of being a pop star, attending gigs regularly and bending the ears of any famous musicians who'd let him. His interest in art consisted of producing endless drawings of his hero Jimi Hendrix.

To his friends, Freddie was a contradictory figure – one moment appearing shy and insecure, and the next boasting about his imminent superstardom. Inspired by Brian and Tim, he began jamming with Nigel Foster and Chris Smith – the latter having been dismissed from Smile due to his overly-bluesy style of playing. The three friends would make a racket deep into the night, Freddie pounding the piano and bemoaning his inability to write a song as good as Smile's 'Step On Me'. To him, it sounded almost as good as a Beatles number. He also tried to write on guitar, though he could barely play the instrument. The three of them would often have to duck into the nearest guitar shop whenever Freddie was struck by a new song idea. Pretending to be interested in buying a particular instrument, he'd strum it for however long it took to work out his chord sequence, after which he'd hang it back on the wall, much to the annoyance of the shop assistants.

Freddie's compositional efforts – usually arrived at by stitching disconnected ideas together with his odd staccato piano runs ('like Mozart gone mad', in Smith's words) – often led him up blind alleys. When he got really stuck, he'd fall back on the 'Woke up, got out of bed' middle section of The Beatles' 'A Day In The Life'. One song Freddie and Smith *did* manage to get together in a semi-complete form was 'The Real Life' (working title 'The Cowboy Song'), which Smith claims contained the opening line 'Mama just killed a man'. But neither Freddie nor Chris were quite convinced by it, so it was placed on their ever-growing pile of rejects.

Though Freddie hankered to join Smile, they too seemed to be going nowhere fast – a symptom perhaps of their reluctance to give up academia and turn professional. One of their more-notable achievements was impressing Paul McCartney, though this had nothing to do with their music. Falling back on his design training, Tim concocted a grinning-mouth logo, which accompanied all their press releases. Having sent a demo tape to The Beatles' brand new Apple label, Tim and Brian received a note from McCartney saying, 'Love the logo!'. What he made of the tunes on the tape, the two musicians are still waiting to find out.

Smile's sound was largely defined by Brian's distinctive guitar tone and style. While many late-1960s rock guitarists aimed for a loose and raunchy feel, Brian's playing had a more precise, crystalline clarity. He could burn up and down the fretboard with the best of them, but his runs were always articulated with immense care and attention to detail. His homemade instrument also ensured that many of the sounds he made were quite literally unique.

Brian's pulverising volume and power were noted in a *Times* review of Smile's most significant live outing – a support slot with Joe Cocker, Spooky Tooth, The Bonzo Dog Doo-Dah Band and Free at The Royal Albert Hall on 27 February 1969. The review referred to Smile as 'The loudest group in the western world', while forgetting to mention their name. Their set included a memorable Tim Staffell original called 'Earth', which boasted a science-fiction theme and was redolent of David Bowie's 'Space Oddity'. (Tim later dismissed his song as 'pretentious cobblers'.) Roger invited his friend Doug Puddifoot to film part of the Royal Albert Hall performance, which he duly did on black-and-white 8mm tape. It's still the earliest known footage of Brian and Roger in action, but it's without sound.

### Gettin' Smile (Smile EP) (1969)

Personnel:
Brian May: guitar, piano, vocals
Roger Meddows Taylor : percussion, vocals
Tim Staffell: bass, vocals
Producers: John Anthony (Tracks 1, 5, 6); Fritz Fryer (2,3, 4)
Studios: Trident, London, June 1969 (1, 5, 6); De Lane Lea, London, September 1969 (2, 3, 4)
Release date: 1982 (Japan only)
Chart places: Did not chart
Running time: 19:23
Side One: 1. 'Doin' Alright' (May, Staffell), 2. 'Blag' (Taylor), 3. 'April Lady' (Lucas)
Side Two: 1. 'Polar Bear' (May), 2. 'Earth' (Staffell). 3. 'Step On Me (May/Staffell)

In the spring of 1969, Smile managed to get themselves a recording contract with Mercury Records, entering Trident Studios with progressive-rock producer John Anthony, to cut a single. The A-side was 'Earth', backed with 'Step On Me': a bouncy harmony-rich Tim and Brian song from their 1984 days. The ethereal 'Doin' Alright' (another

May/Staffell number), recorded at the same session, was abandoned but not forgotten.

In September, Mercury again paid for Smile to do some recording, this time at De Lane Lea Studios at 129 Kingsway in Holborn. The songs recorded were 'Polar Bear' (a psychedelic reverie with strident vocal pyrotechnics from Tim), 'Blag' (a heavy track featuring harmony scat singing and noisy guitar work, anticipating Brian's 'battalion of riffs' approach on Queen's 'Brighton Rock'), and a cover of the windswept Stanley Lucas ballad 'April Lady', containing Roger's stratospheric vocals. These songs were finally released on the *Gettin' Smile* EP in 1982. Though hardly earth-shattering, the record demonstrates that Brian's unique guitar stylings and the thick harmony vocals later associated with Queen were both key components of Smile's sound. Given that Freddie Bulsara pretty much obliterated Tim Staffell's place in rock history, it's interesting to note that Tim was no mean vocalist himself, with as impressive a range and emotional a delivery as Freddie was able to muster on Queen's debut LP.

In autumn 1969, Smile's final recording session took place at Pye Studios, courtesy of maintenance engineer Terry Yeadon, who Brian's girlfriend (and later wife) Christine 'Chrissie' Mullen had introduced to him. Yeadon and disc cutter Geoff Calvar convened an illicit post-midnight session at Pye, simply to give themselves some producing experience. They recorded new versions of 'Polar Bear' and 'Step On Me', but given that Yeadon and Calvar had no real clout in the music industry, this was little more than an exercise. Terry – who at least was able to give the band an acetate to shop around – later told *Record Collector*: 'I was impressed by their sound. Roger might've been a little rough at first, but Brian had a guitar tone identical to the one he used in Queen'. Though they didn't know it, Terry and Geoff hadn't seen the last of Brian and Roger.

It would've been neater had Smile's career ended at the end of 1969 – clearing the way for Brian, Roger and Freddie Bulsara's new band to rise magically from the ashes. But the story was to be a little more complicated than that.

# 1970 – Build Your Own Boat

Freddie and Roger had become best buddies. They were also now flatmates in a rambling crash pad at 40 Ferry Road in Barnes, West London. As dedicated followers of fashion, the two long-haired students were often seen parading around town, decked out in floral brilliance, crushed velvet and outlandish satin. They'd even gone into business together, running an art and antiques stall in Kensington Market, with Freddie's Hendrix artwork prominently on display. They then decided they'd make more money selling vintage clothing – most of it cast-offs salvaged from charity shops and disreputable street vendors. Slade's Noddy Holder later recalled buying his famed mirror hat from the stall. Most of their custom came from the many bohemians, eccentrics and hippies who frequented the area. Roger has said that many of the young men on the scene were either gay or pretending to be, and that this may have been influential on Freddie's decision to propose a certain band name later that year.

Having now abandoned his dentistry studies, Roger was still hopeful of success with Smile. But despite their best efforts, they finally ran out of steam. Brian's continuing postgraduate research into zodiacal light took him in early 1970 to the slopes of a dormant volcano in Tenerife. This blew a hole in Smile's gigging schedule and caused them to lose momentum. Then on 29 March, Tim announced he was leaving the band to pursue different musical avenues with a folk rock group called Humpy Bong. Brian and Roger could've called time on their musical partnership at this point, but a certain friend of theirs had other ideas. Roger told broadcaster Bob Harris in 1977: 'Freddie took us in hand. He told us, 'Come on, you can't give up. I wanna sing!''.

Over the previous few months, Freddie had been busy. For a start, he'd acquired a cheap guitar, and tried to expand his knowledge of chord progressions. He was now managing to write full songs on guitar and piano, bouncing back and forth between heavy rock and classical-flavoured pop. Having struggled for a long time to produce anything to rival Brian and Tim's Smile efforts, Freddie had begun piecing together melodies that had their own individual stamp. For a time, he also joined a band called Ibex, which – though coming from St. Helens, Merseyside – shared a social scene with Smile courtesy of some mutual friends from Imperial College. It was with Ibex (which Freddie later re-named Wreckage) that he began striking the theatrical poses that would become his trademark. During one gig, he accidentally snapped off the base of his microphone stand but continued singing with the mic still attached to the upper *boom* section. This became known as Freddie's stick: a prop he'd brandish and cavort with on stage for the rest of his career.

Ibex/Wreckage eventually fell apart, leaving a disconsolate Freddie to begin the new decade making the rounds of various design agencies in the hope of picking up freelance employment. He took on a commission from the Austin Knight company, to provide drawings for a women's corset advertisement. Other scattered jobs included illustrating for a children's science-fiction book and another about World War I aircraft. But none of these jobs scratched Freddie's creative itch, and he continued obsessing over becoming a pop star.

A stint singing in the band Sour Milk Sea conferred precious little rock-'n'-roll glory. That band's founder member Chris Dummett recalled Freddie had long coveted the role of Smile lead vocalist. Though he'd never done anything to undermine Tim Staffell, Freddie was keenly anticipating the day when Tim would leave and *he* could make his move. Having long been Smile's keenest champion and sternest critic, Freddie finally convinced Roger and Brian that his ideas (and, more importantly, his singing) could catapult them to the big time.

Though it would be convenient to clearly demarcate between the careers of Smile and the nascent Queen, the truth is rather less tidy. For a start, after Staffell left, Brian and Roger (with Mike Grose – a Cornish bassist and the owner of a Truro club called PJ's) played several Smile gigs without a singer, persuading Staffell to return for a couple of shows in April and May. However, there are eye-witness accounts of Freddie onstage with May, Taylor and Grose at the PJ's club in the spring of 1970. It might've been that Brian and Roger were auditioning Freddie in a live setting while also keeping their options open. In later years, Brian admitted he'd been far from convinced of Freddie's vocal talents. He told YouTube's Rick Beato: 'His role in Wreckage had been to run around and scream his head off. He was actually a frightening lead singer – very loud, in your face and insistent. Roger and I didn't take to it at first'.

Freddie's onstage personality evolved slowly. He was a very different frontman to Tim – slinking around the stage with black nail varnish prominently on display, and striking dramatic poses with his *stick*. But early witnesses remember him seeming nervous at times, and he wasn't always able to command an audience. Vocally, he wasn't there yet either, his voice occasionally breaking into a peculiar vibrato which Roger later likened to 'a very powerful sheep'. However, Freddie saw his limitations not as problems but as challenges to overcome.

Having muscled his way into the band, he now decided they needed a new name. Ignoring the others' suggestions – which included The Great Dance, Rich Kids and – most improbably – Build Your Own Boat, his suggestion (made in the garden at 40 Ferry Road) was Queen. It was a word perfectly expressing the regal, feminine glamour he felt the group should now possess. (In later years, Wreckage bassist John 'Tupp' Taylor claimed credit for the new name, given that he'd always referred to Freddie affectionately as 'the old queen'.) The name Queen was suggestive of pomp and ceremonial splendour, characteristics that would become inseparable from the band. But of course, there was also the sexual connotation.

Despite boasting androgynous looks themselves, Brian and Roger were united in being unsure about the name Queen (visually so similar to the then-still-pejorative 'queer'). They were worried the homosexual overtone wouldn't curry universal favour. But Freddie was adamant. He told *People* magazine in 1977: 'The whole point of the name was to be provocative, to prompt speculation and controversy.' Significantly, around this time, some of Freddie's friends had begun speculating that he was conflicted about his *own* sexuality. Despite his natural shyness, he'd long projected a personality that could best be described as camp. He'd been known to date women, but according to some of his friends of the period, he was spending an increasing amount of time in the company of gay men. It's unknown if his idea to call the band Queen was an expression of his emerging bisexuality, but it doesn't take a huge leap of imagination to find that theory compelling. At any rate, he won the argument over the band name.

Confusingly, the gig now universally accepted as Queen's first, was billed using the name Smile. This was at Truro City Hall on 27 June, and promoted by the British Red Cross Society as presenting an unmissable opportunity to 'come and DANCE'. Mike Grose remembers the band all wearing black velvet trousers, black t-shirts and stack-heeled boots at Freddie's insistence. The singer had also raided a friend's jewellery box, and was dripping in bracelets and other glittering accoutrements. Later, the band drove back to London in Grose's van, with an excited Freddie talking non-stop about the show for the entire journey.

The next gig was on 18 July at Imperial College, London. A surviving ticket stub testifies that this time the band was billed as Queen.

Brian later recalled how exciting it was playing at this venue, given the number of times he'd attended as a punter. The Imperial show is historically significant in having produced the first-known live images of Queen: courtesy of Roger's friend Doug Puddifoot. The black-and-white and rather-indistinct photos suggest a dark, enigmatic image was part of the band's DNA from the beginning.

A new Freddie song called 'Liar' was introduced at Queen's next gig (this one billed as 'Queen (formerly Smile)' at Truro's PJ's club on 25 July. This show was recorded onto two reel-to-reel tapes by a friend of Mike Grose, and turned out to be the bassist's final outing. He was duly replaced by a Harrow department-store salesman called Barry Mitchell – a recommendation from one of Roger's Cornwall friends. Barry made his debut appearance at Imperial Lecture Theatre A on 23 August. He later recalled nearly being put off staying in the band when – half an hour before his first gig – Freddie suddenly seized on the idea that they should all play the concert in drag. Fortunately, he was talked out of it, and went on in an open-topped, black one-piece fitted with wing-like protuberances on the cuffs and ankles: an outfit designed by his friend Wendy Edmonds from the market stall,

On 18 September, Freddie and Roger closed their Kensington Stall at lunchtime out of respect for their mutual hero Jimi Hendrix, whose death in a London hotel an hour or so before had just been announced on the news. Having intended to spend that evening rehearsing new material, the band instead played Hendrix tunes. Jimi's death was devastating for Freddie. Having once described Hendrix as 'just a beautiful man, a master showman and a dedicated musician', he'd plastered the walls of his dank bedroom with Hendrix posters, and regularly scoured the country, catching him live whenever he could. Perhaps even more than Jimi's fantastic music – the elaborate textures of which Freddie would later strive to equal – Freddie had been drawn to Hendrix's androgynous image, exotic dress sense and sexualised stage moves. These would all have an incalculable influence on the creation of Freddie's on-stage (and ultimately all-consuming) alter ego.

Freddie Bulsara informally changed his name to Freddie Mercury shortly after Queen's formation – possibly even after the first Truro City Hall gig on 27 June. According to Brian, after Freddie wrote his early song 'My Fairy King' (which features a heartfelt plea to Mother Mercury), he announced, 'I am going to become Mercury, as the mother in this song is *my* mother'. He later claimed that the name had been inspired by reading about the Roman god Mercury: messenger of the gods. (Intriguingly, Mercury was also the God of financial gain!) A more subliminal association might've been with the liquid element otherwise known as Quicksilver, which the ancient Chinese and Tibetans believed possessed great healing properties (it's actually poisonous), or, of course, with the planet closest to the sun. Taken together, these three inspirations suggested mythological antiquity, heavenly power and celestial communication, bodily healing and destruction, and proximity to indescribably-high physical temperatures. On a more mundane level, in an era of pop stars with glam pseudonyms like Gary Glitter and Alvin Stardust, the name Freddie Mercury just sounded cool.

As with everything Freddie and the band did, the decisions to adopt the names Queen and Freddie Mercury were calculated to achieve a specific effect; unlike in the Smile days, nothing was being left to chance. The visual and lexical concepts underpinning the group's identity were now in place, and it simply remained to sell them to the world.

# 1971-1972 – Downtime

Queen started 1971 with a date on 8 January at the famous Marquee in Wardour Street. In Ewell the next evening, they joined another scuffling band called Genesis, supporting Kevin Ayres and The Whole World. In the dressing room after the show, Genesis singer Peter Gabriel approached Roger and told him Genesis were shortly going to be needing a new drummer, and asked if he'd be interested in auditioning. Roger politely declined. (The subsequent audition was attended by Phil Collins, who, of course, got the job). The Ewell gig was also notable for being the final outing for Barry Mitchell, who'd decided that Freddie's vocal limitations were holding Queen back. He was also full of doubt about the group's musical direction, feeling it was too derivative of prog-rockers Yes.

Ironically, Barry's successor Doug Bogie (an 18-year-old trainee telephone engineer), joined Queen just in time for a February support slot with Yes at Kingston Polytechnic. Unfortunately, this concert was memorable for all the wrong reasons. Wanting to show off to a bunch of his friends who'd come to watch, the new bassist got a little carried away, jumping up and down and cavorting around in what Brian later described (with admirable restraint) as a 'most incongruous manner'. Doug was quietly let go.

A few days later, Roger and Brian attended a disco at the Maria Assumpta Teacher Training college – an event that most Queen histories state was their first meeting with bassist and Chelsea College undergraduate John Deacon. John had seen Queen play the previous October, though he later admitted they hadn't made much of an impression. Having accepted Brian and Roger's offer to audition, he turned up the following week at Imperial College, armed with a rather tasty Rickenbacker bass and a tiny homemade amp that the others christened The Deacy Amp. Unlike his three predecessors, John somehow gave the impression that he was going to be *the one*. Roger explained in a 1977 Radio 1 interview: 'We all really liked him because he was different from us. We were so used to each other and were so over the top, and we thought because he was so quiet, he'd fit right in without any trouble'.

John Richard Deacon (or Easy Deacon as he'd been nicknamed in his teens) had always been quiet, right back to his school days in Oadby, Leicestershire. He became an inveterate dabbler in electronics at an early age, throwing together his own radio receiver and recording songs off the radio onto a primitive reel-to-reel tape recorder. In 1963, he was inspired to pick up the acoustic guitar after hearing The Beatles. A couple of years later, he and school friend Nigel Bullen formed The Opposition (later briefly renamed The New Opposition). They played the usual youth clubs and church halls, eventually becoming finalists in the Midlands Beat Championships. Reflecting John's developing tastes, the group started out playing Motown covers before developing a heavy, more rocking sound. By 1969 they'd changed their name to Art, and cut a self-financed single, though no record deal was forthcoming. John called it quits that summer. Moving to London to start his degree, he began looking for a band to play with. Nigel later recalled John telling him he'd usually chicken out from attending auditions if it turned out the group in question had any kind of success or profile: certainly not then an issue with the bottom-of-the-heap Queen.

Along with his deft bass work, John impressed Freddie, Brian and Roger with his amazing grasp of electronics. The Deacy Amp alone became one of his major contributions to the band – its heavily saturated tones eventually ending up on a range of songs, including 'The Fairy Feller's Master-Stroke', 'Bohemian Rhapsody', 'Misfire', 'Good Company' and Brian's immortal version of 'God Save The Queen'. With his love for soul music, John presented an interesting contrast to the hard-rock-loving Brian and Roger, and to Freddie, whose taste took in both high-brow and oddball influences such as opera and vaudeville. Though John loved black music, he had no problem playing heavy rock, and soon picked up the changes in Brian's proto-metal potboiler 'Son And Daughter'. Nor was John thrown by an extended blues jam at the end of the audition. In a 1977 TV interview with Bob Harris, John recalled the early rehearsals: 'They'd already decided on the style of music they were doing, and I just slotted into that really'. Nevertheless, in later years, he also claimed it took him a while to find his footing in Queen. Strong bonds of friendship and musical chemistry existed between the other three. Mercury and May, in particular, had begun thinking in unison – Freddie dreaming up operatic vocal arrangements and Brian nurturing grand dreams of overdubbed guitar orchestras. For a Marvin Gaye and Stevie Wonder fan like John, this wasn't exactly familiar territory.

The Queen lineup stabilised at a crucial moment in British pop history. The new glam rock movement had re-energised the teen market, ushering in a new era of buoyant three-minute singles by artists who were less concerned with appearing earnest and authentic, and more interested in outrageous fashion and provocative sexuality. In retrospect, it's clear that Queen were going to fit smoothly into this new scene. Freddie's uniquely regal (queenly) take on glamour was an idea of stunning simplicity and originality, and he passionately believed it would usher in a great future for the band.

It was in this period that much of the music that later appeared on the first two Queen albums began to take shape. A lot of this material had a strong slant towards fantasy and magic – most obviously in Freddie songs like 'My Fairy King' and 'Ogre Battle'. Given that only a couple of years earlier, he'd been bashing the Imperial College piano and bemoaning his lack of songwriting talent, he'd come a very long way in a short amount of time.

Having accepted constructive criticism from the others about his wavering vocals, Freddie also started training his voice, and made rapid progress. Quite unlike the gruff or screeching voices of many contemporaneous singers, his was beginning to take on an operatic quality while somehow retaining more than a vestige of rock-'n'-'roll rawness. It was a unique combination, and was now producing hair-raising results.

The on-stage persona 'Freddie Mercury' had also evolved since the early Truro days. As a fan of Led Zeppelin, Freddie had borrowed something of Robert Plant's fey hippie charm, mixing it with a dose of Hendrix flamboyance, and adding an ironic dash of Satanic majesty. Then there were the catty cabaret elements courtesy of his enthusiasm for theatrical singers like Liza Minnelli. This was all filtered through Freddie's own personality: the preening dandy of Kensington Market. Having long referred to friends and acquaintances as his 'darlings', it seemed a natural step to begin referring to his audiences that way also.

1970 hadn't exactly been awash with live appearances, and 1971 was to be only marginally busier, with several months devoted to intense rehearsal in order to break John into the band. His first live appearance was at Surrey College on 2 July – a date that's since become enshrined in Queen lore as the one where Freddie took exception to John's dress sense and insisted on lending him a shirt for the performance.

Subsequently, the group headed down to Cornwall to play some shows, capitalising on Roger's Truro fame to promote a series of club dates in Hayle, Wadesbridge and Penzance. The informal tour ended on 21 August with Queen's first-ever open-air concert – at Tregye Country Club, on the bill for the Carnon Downs Festival. From there, it was back to London.

Now that the new lineup was up and running, the band decided that their days of playing small pubs and clubs were over. They'd slogged their way around the circuit with Smile, Ibex and Sour Milk Sea, and it had led nowhere. Besides, as Brian said, that was what every other band did, and Queen didn't want to be like every other band.

By now, Roger had started a biology degree, largely because he needed the student grant to help put food on the table. John was still working diligently towards his electronics MSc and would graduate before the year's end. Brian was teaching part-time at a local comprehensive school while continuing to tinker with his astronomy thesis. As free-spirited as ever, Freddie was somehow still scraping by – his penniless situation made more-bearable by his having fallen in love with Mary Austin: a floor manager at the London fashion emporium Biba.

Freddie and Roger had now given up their clothes stall. But as autumn descended, Freddie took on a part-time job selling hand-crafted boots in the shop of Alan Mair: a friend who happened to know David Bowie. Freddie had been an ardent Bowie fan in the latter's early, unsuccessful career phase, and was thrilled when the great man walked into the shop one day and asked for a pair of boots. Despite having finally become a pop star with his 1969 single 'Space Oddity', Bowie confessed he was too skint to pay for the merchandise. Laughingly telling Mair that the music industry was a 'fucked up place', Bowie charmed Mair into getting Freddie to rustle him up a pair of boots *on the house*. For Freddie, who still wore shoes with holes in them, the encounter was a sobering reminder that even with a hit record, you could still end up flat-broke.

While Freddie was giving free boots to Bowie, Brian was re-establishing contact with the Pye Studios technicians Terry Yeadon and Geoff Calvar. The pair were now working at De Lane Lea Studios, and were helping to fit out their new premises at Engineers Way, Wembley. In the process of soundproofing the building's studios, Terry and Geoff needed a loud band to help them test for leakage. In return, they offered to record free demos for any group willing to give their time. This offer was too good for Queen to refuse. By now, they'd worked up several exciting original numbers, and under the guidance of De Lane Lea engineer Louis Austin and his assistant Martin Birch, they used a succession of late-night sessions to cut demos of three Freddie songs ('Liar', 'Jesus' and 'Great King Rat') and two by Brian ('Keep Yourself Alive' and 'The Night Comes Down'). As exciting as it was for them to set up and play in the mini-amphitheatre of De

Lane Lea's Studio 2, they had to endure being moved from one room to another as the sound testing continued. Also, problems with the studio's new tape recorder led to many abortive takes. Despite these issues, the recordings came together surprisingly well. Playing through a wall of Marshall amplifiers procured by Yeadon and Calvar, Brian soon discovered that Birch (later to find fame as a high-profile heavy metal producer) was sympathetic when it came to orchestrating Queen's panoply of guitar textures. From the evidence of the demos, Birch also had sympathy with the band's wish that Roger's drums go down on tape with some lively room ambience.

Listening to the De Lane Lea demos all these years later, it's remarkable how closely the songs resemble the full-blown versions released on Queen's debut album. 'Keep Yourself Alive' – though featuring its central riff played on acoustic guitar – is largely all there, with Freddie's overlapping vocal lines already hard-baked into the arrangement. The complex musical architecture of 'Great King Rat' – with its interweaving, bludgeoning electric riffs and acoustic Flamenco flourishes – is negotiated with pin-sharp accuracy. So impressive was the version of 'The Night Comes Down', the recording was later included on the first LP – thus becoming the earliest Queen recording to be officially released.

Austin later remembered the band as fussy and fastidious, insisting on doing endless takes until the sound they heard in their heads had been transferred onto tape. By all accounts, it was Freddie who was most hard on himself. At the outset of the recording, Yeadon recalled him striking shapes in the studio as he sang, parading about with his *stick* as if he was performing at a concert. As a result, his vocal takes were frequently off-key, with some words or phrases disappearing off-mic.

One afternoon towards the end of their time at De Lane Lea, Queen received an impromptu visit from two young Trident Studios producers. Most accounts agree that the visitors were Roy Thomas Baker and John Anthony – the latter being the respected prog producer who'd shepherded into existence such albums as Genesis' *Trespass* and Van der Graaf Generator's *Pawn Hearts*. Anthony had worked with Brian and Roger before, on the 1969 Smile session at Trident. Since then, he'd kept in touch and knew that Smile had morphed into Queen. He and Baker had ostensibly popped in to check out a new mixing desk at the request of Trident owner Norman Sheffield. But given that Anthony was now doing some A&R work for Trident Audio Productions, it's possible he was also surreptitiously checking out the band.

Anthony and Baker were impressed by the demos-in-progress, spiriting away copies to play to Sheffield. Meanwhile, wanting to keep all options open, Queen recruited their friend and former Ibex manager, Ken Testi, to begin the unenviable task of knocking on record company doors. Ironically, the band themselves couldn't listen to the tapes, as none of them could afford a reel-to-reel machine. Legend has it that they eventually borrowed one from Genesis keyboardist Tony Banks.

At the beginning of 1972, Queen received some interest from Genesis and Lindisfarne manager Tony Stratton-Smith of Charisma Records. But after some deliberation, Queen turned down his offer of £20,000, a new van and a tour of Belgium in favour of a counteroffer from Trident Audio Productions. By the early-1970s, Trident had established itself as one of the most well-loved and prestigious recording facilities in the country. Nestled in the quiet St. Anne's Court alleyway just off Wardour Street in the heart of Soho, Trident had played host to The Beatles, David Bowie, T. Rex and a host of others. Sibling bosses Norman and Barry Sheffield had equipped the studio with the finest equipment they could get their hands on, including one of the first 8-track recorders in Europe – which was soon upgraded to a 16-track machine. They were also in the process of branching out into other areas of the music industry. Their new company Trident Audio Productions was an innovative attempt to amalgamate record production, song publishing and artist management under one umbrella.

John Anthony had strong-armed Norman into listening to Queen's De Lane Lea demos. But it was Barry who finally decided the group was worth pursuing, having caught them live at a nursing-college dance on 24 March and been blown away by their audacious cover of the Broadway show tune 'Big Spender'. When Freddie and the boys trooped into the Sheffields' office a few days later, Norman quickly realised this was no bunch of wet-behind-the-ears hopefuls. Though Norman immediately took to Brian and Roger, he was less sure about Freddie, who he later described in his memoir as 'volatile'.

Sheffield wanted to put Queen through their paces in the studio before offering them a deal. But this would mostly happen in the wee small hours when other acts weren't using the facilities. Brian later recalled that it was galling having to squeeze past various musicians on the stairwell – the likes of David Bowie and Lou Reed on their way up while Brian and the boys made their way down, to drink desultory cups of tea in the café across the road.

Behind the scenes, American music executive Jack Nelson agreed to manage Queen on Trident's behalf. But what Jack needed was product to sell, and so, the sessions segued into the painstaking recording of the band's debut album. Production was undertaken by Roy Thomas Baker and John Anthony. But as spring gave way to summer, the latter bailed out after coming down with a virus. Baker – who'd earned his stripes as a classical engineer at Decca prior to working on such Trident-recorded hits as Free's 'All Right Now' and T. Rex's 'Get It On' – impressed Queen with his technical expertise and air of natural authority. He worked in smooth symbiosis with staff engineers Mike Stone, Ted Sharpe, Ken Scott and David Hentschel. The mastering engineer assigned to Queen was Howard Thompson, who couldn't stand the band's music and didn't mind saying so. He later recalled, with a certain withering clarity, that during the sessions, most of the engineers ended up calling each other Dearie, having picked up the word from Freddie.

These sessions provide the earliest anecdotal accounts of Queen's fiery and tempestuous working relationships. In Norman Sheffield's memoir *Life on Two Legs*, he paints an alarming picture of plates and glasses being hurled across the studio as tempers flared – usually thanks to conflicts between Freddie, Brian and Roger. (Easy Deacon was mouse-like and pretty much invisible.) At first, Norman found these outbreaks alarming, though, in time, he began to realise the arguments were rarely personal and always rooted in artistic differences. Blowups could happen at the drop of a plectrum and arose out of heated discussions about some tiny and seemingly-insignificant detail of a song's arrangement.

One area of contention was the album's drum sound. In the early-1970s, many studios and technicians had adopted the technique of muffling drum kits as much as possible: a trick pioneered by The Beatles in 1968. The Trident engineers were very keen on this, and indeed the Trident drum sound (perhaps most represented on Bowie's album *The Man Who Sold the World*) had become one of the studio's sonic calling cards. The problem was Queen hated it. Brian later revealed in a VH1 interview: 'Roy Thomas Baker would put sticky tape and bits of foam all over the kit, which was stuck in this little booth. It made the drums sound like tissue paper. When we tried to argue, he'd tell us he'd fix it later with some echo, which of course, never works'.

Most bands record their first album quickly and are given more time to produce their second. In Queen's case, they'd already written and rehearsed most of the second LP's material, and had meticulously evolved their sound. They were worried that their debut album would sound dated, especially as they were only too conscious of the fast-evolving music scene beyond the studio walls.

By the summer of 1972, Slade, Gary Glitter and The Sweet were carving up the charts, competing with the previously unassailable Marc Bolan to be the kingpins of glam. Though many of The Sweet's songs were written for them by the backroom team of Nicky Chinn and Mike Chapman, that band were innovative in the way they melded heavy guitars with pop hooks and stacked complex vocal harmonies: Queen's own fast-evolving recipe, in a nutshell. More alarmingly, if Freddie had ever nursed hopes that his feminine costumes and ambiguous sexuality would place him at the cutting edge of rock, he now had to reckon with the stratospheric second coming of Bowie. When Queen went to check him out at London's Rainbow Theatre, they became even more morose.

In the empty hours between recording sessions, Freddie took on some extracurricular musical activity courtesy of Trident staff producer Robin Cable. The latter had begun experimenting in an adjacent studio with the old Ronettes song 'I Can Hear Music'. Cable's idea was to replicate maverick American producer Phil Spector's trademark wall of sound. The resulting record was surprisingly effective, with Freddie's double-tracked lead vocals demonstrating that he was now a talent to be reckoned with (although he's a little flat on Goffin and King's 'Goin' Back' on the B-side). Roger's castanets and tambourine are tastefully performed on 'I Can Hear Music', and in retrospect, Brian's piercing lead lines towards the end scream out 'Queen!'. Norman Sheffield deemed the finished record an artistic success, releasing it the following year under the corny name 'Larry Lurex' (a pastiche of 'Gary Glitter'). Though the single sold in miniscule quantities, it would, of course, one day become an expensive rarity.

That autumn, Freddie also found time to design a magnificent logo and regal emblem for Queen. As his starting point, he used the royal UK coat of arms, then gave free rein to his love of mythology by incorporating a huge phoenix with splayed wings: the symbol of immortality. In place of the traditional design's quartered shield was an ornate Q, inside of which nestled a crown. This was topped with a crab (representing Brian's star sign Cancer), flanked on either side by a pair of crowned lions (for Leos John and Roger) and a duo of seated fairies (for Virgo Freddie himself). With various modifications, this design appeared on Queen releases and merchandise throughout the 1970s.

In typical Freddie fashion, it was a symbol of immense grandiosity and self-importance.

After months of deliberation, Queen had now signed a comprehensive management, recording and publishing deal with Trident. The distinguished music-publishing company B. Feldman & Co. (shortly to be taken over by EMI) agreed to partner up on the publishing, thanks to the intervention of managing director Ronnie Beck who was a great admirer of the band. Beck's generous publishing deal helped Queen upgrade their equipment, though Norman Sheffield's control of the purse strings limited the members' weekly salaries to a measly £20 each.

As a deal sweetener, Norman arranged a 6 November showcase gig at the massive Pheasantry pub on the King's Road in Chelsea. He also promised it would be packed to the rafters with industry bigwigs. Given that Queen had hardly gigged at all in 1972, a high-stakes industry showcase concert at the end of the year wasn't the clever idea it had first seemed. The performance – for which John Deacon and road manager/ electronics whizz John Harris designed and rigged up a new PA system – was an anticlimax, with not a single A&R person turning up. *And* the PA broke down.

A further show at The Marquee, on 20 December, was the scene of Queen's first encounter with Jac Holzman: president of the hip American record label Elektra. He'd heard the De Lane Lea demo courtesy of Jack Nelson, and it had blown him away. But his first Queen show left him – in his own words – 'dreadfully disappointed'. Before leaving the country, he wrote a five-page memo to Norman Sheffield, setting out in minute detail how the band would need to improve before he'd agree to sign them. It wasn't an outright 'no', but it still felt considerably way-off a 'yes'.

As desperate as Queen had been to end the year on a high, they were left feeling that fame and fortune might be an ever-receding mirage.

# 1973 (Part One) - Top Fax, Pix and Info

Early in 1973, Ronnie Beck rolled a six when – at a huge music industry fair in Cannes – he passed a tape of the Queen album onto EMI executive Roy Featherstone. Featherstone later claimed he'd listened to hundreds of tapes that weekend and had been bored to death by them all. Throwing on the Queen reel, he was jerked from his stupor, and quickly telephoned Trident to signal his interest in signing the band.

While EMI's A&R machinery clanked away, Queen were busy recording for the BBC. Feldman's chief plugger Phil Reed had sweet-talked Bernie Andrews – producer of the BBC Radio 1 show *Sounds of the Seventies* – into giving Queen a four-song session to be broadcast on 15 February. Recorded at the BBC's Langham 1 studio in Portland Place on 5 February, they played blistering versions of 'Keep Yourself Alive', 'Liar', the old Smile number 'Doing Alright' (the missing 'g' of 'Doing' now in place, and its last verse beautifully sung by Roger) and a rendition of Freddie's fairy-tale fantasia 'My Fairy King'.

The session got a positive reaction, further nudging EMI towards giving the band a deal. The company finally pulled the trigger in March, agreeing to distribute Queen records via their new EMI label imprint. But because Queen had signed a prior contract with the Sheffield brothers, they legally remained Trident recording artists. This gave Norman the status of intermediary between band and record company: an arrangement destined to create bad blood further down the line.

To celebrate the new deal, Norman organised another concert at the Marquee for 9 April. Having not played live since December, the group felt the pressure piling on, especially as Elektra boss Jac Holzman was again going to be in attendance. They needn't have worried, for this show was a triumph – Holzman shouting as he left: 'I've seen the future of pop music, and it's a band called Queen!'. Elektra promptly offered a US distribution deal.

After what felt like infinitely-protracted backroom wrangling, EMI finally released the first Queen single on 6 July: 'Keep Yourself Alive' b/w 'Son and Daughter'. The US release followed in October. Given that May and Taylor later admitted that Freddie was the strongest writer in the early days, it's interesting that two *Brian* songs were chosen. Perhaps it was because they complemented each other so well, with the poppy, sing-along A-side shadowed by the rather doomy Black Sabbath-like flipside. This melding of tuneful pop and heavy guitar riffing set the template for much of Queen's music over the next five years.

Despite a blaze of publicity from Trident, 'Keep Yourself Alive' picked up little airplay. Radio 1 rejected it no fewer than five times, claiming it took too long to get going. But some press reviews were positive – *The Daily Mirror* describing it as 'a diabolical, high-energy nerve tingler'. But *Disc* magazine was less kind, calling Queen's sound 'genteel' and too derivative of Hendrix and The Who. John Peel's complimentary write-up in *Sounds* was double-edged, for he described the song as featuring 'pleasing guitar and synthesizer work'. This needled Brian, who'd decided early on that all the band's futuristic sound manipulations would be achieved through the complex layering of his Red Special guitar. Such was his determination to highlight the absence of synths on Queen records, it became a regular disclaimer in their LP liner notes for the next three years.

## Queen (1973)

Personnel:
Freddie Mercury: vocals, piano
Brian May: guitars, piano, vocals
Deacon John: bass
Roger Meddows Taylor: percussion, vocals
Producers: John Anthony, Roy Thomas Baker, Queen
Additional recording credit for 'The Night Comes Down': Louis Austin
Studios: De Lane Lea, London, September-December 1971; Trident, London, January 1972-January 1973
Release dates: UK: 13 July 1973, US: 4 September 1973
Chart places: Did not chart on its original release. Later peaked in the UK at 42 (1974), 49 (1975) and 24 (1976). Peaked at 83 in the US in 1974
Running time: 38:49
Side One: 1. 'Keep Yourself Alive' (May), 2. 'Doing Alright' (May, Staffell), 3. 'Great King Rat' (Mercury), 4. 'My Fairy King' (Mercury)
Side Two: 1. 'Liar' (Mercury), 2. 'The Night Comes Down' (May), 3. 'Modern Times Rock 'N' Roll' (Taylor), 4. 'Son And Daughter' (May), 5. 'Jesus' (Mercury), 6. 'Seven Seas Of Rhye...' (Mercury)

After Queen had mercifully rejected the album working titles *Top Fax, Pix & Info* (Roger's suggestion) and *Dearie Me* (no one took credit for that), the debut LP finally arrived titled *Queen*. The record was housed in an eye-catching cover showing a manipulated Doug Puddifoot photo from the 20 December Marquee show. It showed Freddie standing on stage in a heroic *rock superstar* pose, bathed in two spotlights. Brian later explained that the image was supposed to create the impression of the singer as a figurehead on the bow of an old sailing ship. From the start, Queen was a democratic band with no conventional leader – in fact, Freddie was adamant about this. But it's significant that he alone was on the front cover and in such an iconic pose. His majestic Queen logo adorned the front jacket, his crown design perched within the letter Q. For the back cover (which featured Freddie's star-sign-themed emblem), Doug pieced together a somewhat-jumbled collage of band photos – some from the Marquee gig, but many from a riotous fancy-dress party held in June 1971 at the Fulham apartment of Roger's friend Les Brown. (Some John Deacon shots therefore predate his first gig with the band.) There were also photos taken in Freddie and Mary's home.

It's clear from the snaps that the band chose not to project their usual dark and mysterious image. One photo shows a semi-nude Roger grinning coquettishly with a flower in his mouth, while Brian is pictured in a penguin costume! John was credited as Deacon John, as the others felt this made him sound more like a rock star. Roger's credit was his full name Roger Meddows Taylor , again to create a grand impression. In addition to the soon-to-be-familiar disclaimer, 'Nobody played synthesizer', the liner notes were careful to acknowledge that the music represented 'at last something of what Queen music has been over the last three years'. The subtext was clear – the band were aggrieved at how long it had taken to get the album out and worried it wasn't a true showcase of their current sound.

Despite their misgivings, *Queen* is a spirited piece of work, which – a few sonic issues aside – still stands up today. Though at the time it was accused of borrowing too heavily from Led Zeppelin and Yes, those influences aren't all that conspicuous. There's more than a hint of Hendrix, of course, along with Black Sabbath's Tony Iommi in the heavier guitar tones. But the uniquely-cutting qualities of the Red Special are a constant reminder that we're listening to Queen and no one else. The band is already operating as a tight unit, with the rhythm section providing a sturdy platform on which Freddie and Brian weave their melodic fantasies. Freddie's voice – though lacking his later operatic power – punches through the mix with clarity and melodic agility. Roger, on the other hand, suffers beneath the muted thud of the famous Trident drum sound.

The record begins with 'Keep Yourself Alive' – a turbo-charged anthem with heavily phased, harmonised guitars and overlapping vocal phrases. Despite its metallic overtones, it highlights the band's flair for creating earworms. Unusually for a Brian composition, the song is entirely constructed of major chords, and the lyric is upbeat and mischievous. It takes a sideways glance at the foibles of fame and fortune, with the singer's friends and family calling on him to seek a path to glory. The chorus reveals in no uncertain terms that staying alive is probably as worthy a goal as any other. An undoubted Queen classic, the track features the splendid artillery fire of Roger's drum solo, which sounds like The Surfaris' Ron Wilson on steroids.

The May/Staffell song 'Doing Alright' is rendered with exquisite tenderness in its opening piano sections. (Incidentally, the piano was the Trident Bechstein used on The Beatles' 'Hey Jude'.) Roger's intense falsetto gives the vocal harmonies a mesmerising texture. May's snarling guitar is a moment of delicious surprise, coming as it does straight out of Roger's Latin bridge groove. This guitar part is also the first proper clue that Queen would have something serious to offer the world of hard rock and possibly even heavy metal.

Freddie's 'Great King Rat' is – in sequencing terms at least – his first contribution to a Queen album. This edifice of brutal riffs and simmering Flamenco-inspired passages contains several complex interlocking movements: a clear precursor to the next album's experiments. The lyric is a tip of the hat to the English nursery rhyme 'Old King Cole'. The medieval slant of the storyline and characters also reveals a debt to late-1960s/early-1970s progressive rock.

Side one closes with one of Freddie's most beautiful and enigmatic creations. 'My Fairy King' is nothing less than the musical equivalent of a mosaic, with rich and complex vocal harmonies that would do The Beach Boys proud. Featuring pumping Freddie piano and Roger's extraordinary vocal screams, the song is believed to be Freddie's attempt to evoke the magical settings of his childhood home Zanzibar. There are also references to Robert Browning's poem *The Pied Piper of Hamelin*, which also features winged horses, fallow deer and bees which have lost their stings. As impressive as the song is, it peters out at the very moment the listener is expecting a towering climax. It seemed that Freddie's monumental visions weren't quite yet being matched by his ability to express them in epic terms.

The third consecutive Freddie song here is 'Liar' – another bruising rocker which had long been a live staple. With its doomy, Sabbath-like bass solo, the song later cemented Queen's reputation as one of the great heavy bands of the early-1970s. The foreboding mood (anticipating the second album's side black) is enhanced with various church-like elements, including a brooding organ, a call-and-response vocal section and a liturgical lyric in which a sinner mournfully addresses a priest. With its intimations of sin and hopes of redemption, the lyric is a clear precursor to 'Bohemian Rhapsody'.

Brian's 'The Night Comes Down' begins with percussive folk riffs from his 1930s German Hallfredh acoustic guitar, to the accompaniment of a wash of cymbals. The song then blossoms into a mid-tempo ballad which finds the singer bleakly looking back on happier times. Although the line 'Lucy was high' suggests Brian was at least partly thinking of 1967's Summer of Love and The Beatles, the song has a deeper resonance if viewed as a paean to vanished youth. Brian's harmonised Red Special orchestration is a subtle colouring effect, nicely offsetting Freddie's vocal, which often strays into a sweet falsetto. A significant footnote to this song is that it's the De Lane Lea demo, thus the 'recorded by' credit given to Louie Austin.

Though Roger would much later evolve into a highly commercial songwriter, his early efforts tended to plough a more generic rock furrow. 'Modern Times Rock 'N' Roll' features furious guitars, thrashing hi-hats and a lead vocal that borders on the unhinged. Always the Queen member most attached to traditional rock-'n'-roll themes, Roger's references to 'high-heeled boots', 'groovy clothes' and a 'jukebox blowin' no fuse' anticipate the fun hedonism of songs like 'Tenement Funster' and 'Rock It (Prime Jive)'.

Brian's song 'Son And Daughter' begins with a thick swirl of vocal harmonies (Roger's voice high in the mix), before plunging into a sludgy guitar/bass riff, sounding like the progenitor of a million metal bands. Indeed, many heavy artists from the 1980s onward have acknowledged the track as an influence. The lyric deals with intergenerational conflict – a theme that would occupy Brian a lot through the years. The song is notable for being the B-side to the first Queen single, 'Keep Yourself Alive', and for being the first original number that John Deacon learned (at his audition).

The album's final full song is Freddie's 'Jesus', which has a slow, ritualistic feel and another lyric drenched in biblical flavours. Given his background in Zoroastrianism, it's unclear why he was moved to write the song. And in typical Freddie fashion, he never discussed it. Significantly, another Jesus-themed song he wrote called 'Mad The Swine' (originally slated for side one between 'Great King Rat' and 'My Fairy King') was cut because the band felt the album's lyrics were becoming too religious. After 'Jesus', the record comes to a tantalizing conclusion with a quick excerpt from a Freddie song-in-progress called 'Seven Seas Of Rhye…', which is little more than an opening piano fanfare followed by a rapid fade as the band piles in behind.

Though it came as a vast relief to the band that their record was finally on sale, they still felt anxious that it had come too late. By spring 1973, the UK glam rock scene had reached its zenith with the release of David Bowie's *Aladdin Sane*. Other glittery platters by the likes of Roxy Music and Alice Cooper were a little further down the charts. Queen had long feared that by the time they finally emerged onto the scene, music might've moved on and they'd be viewed as imitators. In the event, that's exactly what happened, for as they eased themselves into a batch of live dates to support the LP, some of the music press were quick to express disdain, comparing Queen with supposedly more credible bands like The New York Dolls. It didn't help that EMI's promotional blitz gave the impression that Queen was industry-manufactured. Reports of them arriving at gigs in stretch limos raised hackles among music journalists, particularly those who considered authenticity and paying dues to be a vital part of any young rock group's rise to the top. The band's elaborate lighting rig apparently offered more evidence that they were suffering from serious delusions of grandeur. There were even unkind rumours that Queen had used session musicians on their record – the logic being that any group as glamorous as them couldn't be even remotely talented.

Despite all this, the reviews of *Queen* weren't all terrible. But there were a couple of real clunkers – including an *NME* piece describing the LP as 'a bucket of urine'. Significantly, some of the more-positive notices came from across the pond. In *Rolling Stone* on 12 June, Gordon Fletcher declared, 'There's no doubt that this funky, energetic English quartet has all the tools they'll need to lay claim to the Zep's abdicated heavy-metal throne, and beyond that to become a truly influential force in the rock world. Their debut album is superb'.

Despite their relative lack of profile, the UK music weeklies viewed Queen as attention-worthy. A July *Melody Maker* interview found Freddie anxious to reinforce their mission statement as being 'regal and majestic. Glamour is part of us, and we want to be dandy. We want to shock and be outrageous instantly'.

If a reaction was what the band was looking for, they didn't have to wait too much longer to get it.

# 1973 (Part Two) – Mott is Dead, Long Live Queen!

Though Queen's first album had finally landed, the single was still largely being ignored. Worried that the group's risqué name might be repelling the BBC head honchos, EMI dispatched a copy of the album in a plain white sleeve with a blank label. Mike Appleton (producer) and Bob Harris (presenter), of the popular music TV show *The Old Grey Whistle Test*, both loved the opening track and scheduled it for broadcast. As Appleton had no idea who it was by, he compiled a montage of clips from old black-and-white movie reels – a fun idea, but hardly something that was going to appeal to teenage glam fans. Still, it appeared to do the trick – the BBC switchboard was soon jammed with callers wanting information about the group.

The song's TV debut brought some much-needed exposure the band's way, but it didn't increase the single's airtime or help give it a chart placing. Nor did a hastily-recorded and somewhat-wooden *in-performance* promo video do the trick. Concerned that Queen were perceived as angling themselves exclusively at the albums market Zeppelin-style, Freddie told *Melody Maker*, 'Singles are important to us, and to have a hit now would help the band. We've more to offer than bands like The Sweet'.

A second *Sounds of the Seventies* session – recorded on 25 July (broadcast on 13 August) – caught the band at an unfulfilling juncture in their career. By now they'd written and rehearsed all the second album's material, and were weeks away from recording it. But feeling that the first LP still hadn't gained the exposure it deserved, they decided to showcase its two most significant tunes, 'Keep Yourself Alive' and 'Liar', with Freddie laying down newly-recorded vocal tracks that sounded rawer than his performances on the album cuts. They rounded out the session with an extended 'Son and Daughter', along with the heavy Brian blues number 'See What A Fool I've Been'. Inspired by Sonny Terry and Brownie McGhee's 'That's How I Feel', the song had long been a part of the live set, usually performed as an encore. An historic curio, it demonstrates that Freddie wasn't in his natural element singing the blues. But it *is* a fascinating glimpse into Brian's blues roots, which haven't been acknowledged very much over the years.

By the summer of 1973, Roger had his biology degree, and was finally ready to devote himself full-time to the band. Brian was still dithering with his thesis, and was teaching part-time, though it wouldn't be long before he handed in his notice. Far from convinced that Queen had a viable future, John had begun a postgraduate electronics course. All of the band were still flat broke and anxiously watching the progress of the single and album. But despite their hopes, neither charted at the time.

Throughout August, intensive recording sessions for the new album distracted them from commercial woes. According to Brian, the record's basic premise was to take up the mantle of The Beatles, whose 1967 masterpiece *Sgt. Pepper's Lonely Hearts Club Band* had set a new precedent in complex multitracking. Brian later told VH-1: 'The Beatles were always our bible, but we had access to a lot more technology than they'd had. For the second record, I really wanted to get into layering guitars, and Freddie was thinking along exactly the same lines with the vocals'. Though the debut had hinted at the full Queen sound, the second album snapped it into focus.

The musicians asserted themselves as they'd not been able to the previous year. They dispensed with the services of John Anthony, retaining Roy Thomas Baker in the role of co-producer. Mike Stone – who'd been little more than a Trident teaboy before Queen's arrival – was also brought on board, as the group had been impressed with his remix of 'Keep Yourself Alive' on the first record. Queen were determined that their new album should be recorded with only select elements of the patent Trident sound. This meant rescuing Roger's drums from the tiny booth they'd been crammed into on the first album, and disinterring them from miles of duct tape and foam. Extra care was also taken with microphone placement, ensuring that a lot more room ambience went down on tape.

Baker quickly realised this wasn't going to be just any album. With Freddie arranging monumental six-part harmonies, and Brian hell-bent on creating the world's first virtual electric guitar orchestra (Strictly speaking, Mike Oldfield had already done that with 1973's *Tubular Bells,* though not in a rock-'n'-roll context), Baker knew he had to up his game. 'It was the kitchen sink album' became Roy's most memorable quote – Queen's vaulting ambition forcing him to morph from humble staff producer into sonic wizard and fearless pioneer of multitrack madness. Somehow – against all odds – the album was recorded in one calendar month.

The next major date in the Queen diary – 13 September – came courtesy of their new allies, the BBC. The band were invited to play a concert at the 700-seat North London venue Golders Green Hippodrome, to be recorded and broadcast on national radio on 20 September. The buzz around Queen is clear at this concert, where an excited volley of cheers and whistles follows compere Alan Black's introduction of 'One of the brightest bands around'. The show starts with the prerecorded guitar instrumental 'Procession' (from the coming new album), after which the band explodes onto stage with the new song 'Father To Son'. In retrospect, it's clear Queen were positioning themselves as a band that could straddle the twin worlds of hard and progressive rock: darker than Genesis, artier than Sabbath, more pop than Tull, more glamorous than Yes. Emphasising their roots, they finished the concert with their usual selection of rock-'n'-roll covers, though this encore wasn't broadcast.

Exactly one month after the Hippodrome show, Queen played their first European date at The Underground in Bonn, Germany. After a further gig in Luxembourg, it was back to the UK. The plan was to do a handful of headline dates prior to a longer tour opening for Mott the Hoople – for Queen, the most exciting step up the ladder in their live career so far.

On 2 November, the headlining concert at Imperial College found all four Queen members plastered in mascara at Freddie's insistence. Their stage outfits were outlandish, with John sporting a huge floppy bowtie, a Hawaiian-themed tank top and a wide-sleeved gown inlaid with glittering lightning flashes. The group played well and received a glowing review from *Disc* magazine – courtesy of their soon-to-be-regular champion Rosemary Horide. Also in attendance was renowned photographer Mick Rock, whose work had graced album covers by David Bowie and Syd Barrett. Through his friendship with Bowie, Rock was a true denizen of the UK glam scene, and he recognised a kindred spirit in the androgynous Freddie. Agreeing to do a photo session just before the Mott tour, Rock produced the first iconic set of Queen images – among them, the shots of the band gathered together apparently naked (they were actually just stripped to the waist), wearing feminine makeup and throwing smouldering looks to camera. Thrilled with his work, the band gave Rock an acetate of the new record and asked him to come up with some album-cover ideas.

Having started 1973 as an unsigned band with studio cabin fever, Queen finished the year in style as special guests of Mott the Hoople.

Though the Herefordshire band had recently achieved huge chart success with their single of the Bowie-written 'All The Young Dudes', this had built on their already-fanatical following. Unfortunately, Queen's theatricality wasn't always to the taste of Mott's fans, one of whom took an opportunity to hurl a hot-dog at Freddie in mid-performance. Mott themselves viewed their support act with some bemusement, but Queen loved the headliners' grasp of stagecraft and the bond they enjoyed with their audience. Brian later said that he'd learned a lot by watching them in action.

During a short break from the Mott itinerary, Queen recorded a third BBC session on December 3 – broadcast three days later. It found them consolidating old material and showcasing three songs from their debut album. Their enjoyment of the tour had been somewhat blighted by the continuing non-appearance of their LP and single in the UK charts, so they churned out yet more versions of 'Great King Rat' and 'Son And Daughter', along with Roger's 'Modern Times Rock 'N' Roll': hardly a true representation of their recent musical evolution. At least they were able to debut Freddie's monumental 'Ogre Battle' – a song that pointed to where they were heading next.

On 14 December, the Mott road show climaxed with two gigs in one day at the Hammersmith Odeon. Queen set a record for themselves by performing to 7,000 people across the two performances. Their crossover appeal became visible during these shows, with some youngsters accompanied by grandparents, parents and older siblings. David Bowie attended the evening performance, presumably to see his Mott buddies, though it's tempting to imagine him wanting to check out the singing talents of Freddie Bulsara: the man Bowie had once scavenged a pair of boots from at Kensington Market. Also in attendance was later-to-be Sex Pistols guitarist Steve Jones, who later recalled the gig ending in a near-riot.

That night, Queen presented a huge cake to the Mott the Hoople members as a gesture of thanks for being included on the tour. In recent days, Mott's lead singer Ian Hunter had been getting annoyed by the amount of attention and praise lavished on the support band. He now expressed his feelings rather ungraciously by punching a huge hole in the cake. Perhaps his anxiety was justified – Freddie and Brian later discovered, scrawled in dirt on the side of their coach in the car park, the words 'Mott is dead, long live Queen'. As epitaphs for 1973 went, this one showed distinct promise.

# 1974 (Part One) – Over the Top

Queen began the new year by flying to Australia at the end of January, for a performance at the Sunbury Pop Festival. Staged on private farmland, the event was Australia's answer to the UK's Glastonbury Festival, and Queen were the first non-Australian band ever booked. Things didn't go well. For a start, Brian's arm swelled up after receiving a pre-tour tetanus jab from an unsanitary needle. Then Freddie came down with an ear infection which led to an acute loss of hearing. But this was only the beginning of the band's problems. By now, Queen had begun displaying the control-freak tendencies they were to later become famous for – telling the festival organisers that they wanted to use their own lighting rig and technical team. They also insisted on going onstage later than scheduled, as they didn't want to play in daylight. Given that the festival crew already viewed Queen as foreign interlopers, this didn't go down well. The band ended up at the mercy of a derisive MC, who introduced them as 'a load of limey bastards ... who are probably going to be useless'. Though they turned in a valiant performance, they left the stage to shouts of 'Go back to Pommyland, ya poofters!'. Freddie later dismissed the catcalls, telling a local journalist, 'The next time we come back to Australia, we'll be the biggest band in the world'.

Back in England, the group's growing popularity led to *NME* readers voting them as 'Second Most-Promising Act', after the Dutch group Golden Earring. The paper's rival *Sounds* also declared them 'Third-Best New Band' after Scottish rock bands Nazareth and Blue. The awards were welcome, but in February, the excitement was eclipsed by a sudden invitation to appear on *Top of the Pops*. This wasn't so much a case of the show's producers desperately wanting Queen (whose next single 'Seven Seas Of Rhye' hadn't been released yet), as them urgently needing to plug a gap – Bowie had cancelled at the last minute, and his new promo video for 'Rebel Rebel' wasn't yet ready to be unveiled.

In the early-1970s, *Top of the Pops* was an incredibly influential show. One well-received performance could make an artist a star overnight and propel their record up the charts at breathtaking speed. Remarkably, despite Freddie's insatiable desire to preen in front of the largest audience possible, he was initially resistant to appear and had to be sweet-talked him into it. Queen's *performance* – (As was customary, they were shown miming along to a backing track) – was broadcast on Thursday, 21 February, giving millions of UK viewers their first glimpse of the group. They appeared in their usual sequinned finery – Roger resplendent in silver *Aladdin Sane*-like lightning flashes.

As for the music, 'Seven Seas Of Rhye' was the perfect choice for a single (possibly the *only* sensible choice from the forthcoming album), with its quicksilver piano, shrieking Roger backing vocals, and an exuberant melody couched in layers of distorted guitar. The lyric consisted of a soliloquy delivered by a naked, avenging spirit who'd come to visit terrible destruction on an unspecified race of 'unbelievers'. The song once again had a religious feel, with the singer displaying righteous fury at the sinning ways of the condemned privy counsellors and 'shady senators'. Critics have debated whether the lyric was inspired by the theological writings of Zoroastrianism, but in a 1977 Radio 1 interview, Freddie claimed (as he always did when asked about his inspirations), 'It was fictitious. I wouldn't say surrealistic, but imaginative. I was learning a lot about song structure, and the lyrics were very difficult: quite a task. My strong point is melody – I concentrate on that first, and the lyrics come later'.

February brought two single releases. On the 14th came the USA-only release of 'Liar' b/w 'Doing Alright', which failed to chart, despite its album generating more of a buzz there than in the UK. A week later came the UK release of 'Seven Seas Of Rhye' b/w 'See What A Fool I've Been'. This time, the band's *Top of the Pops* appearance ensured some chart action. In the first week of March, the single entered at 45, climbing steadily over the next few weeks before peaking at ten on 13 April. As Queen celebrated, their second album was already out and selling well. It appeared their fortunes had changed for the better.

### Queen II (1974)

Personnel:
Freddie Mercury: vocals, piano, harpsichord
Brian May: guitar, piano, vocals, bells
John Deacon: bass, acoustic guitar
Roger Meddows Taylor: percussion, vocals
Producers: Roy Thomas Baker, Queen; Robin Geoffrey Cable, Queen ('Nevermore', 'Funny How Love Is'); Roy Thomas Baker, Robin Geoffrey Cable, Queen ('The March Of The Black Queen')
Studio: Trident, August 1973
Release dates: UK: 8 March 1974, US: 9 April 1974
Chart places: UK: 5, US: 49

Running time: 40:51

Side White: 1. 'Procession' (May), 2. 'Father To Son' (May). 3. 'White Queen (As It Began)' (May), 4. 'Some Day One Day' (May), 5. 'The Loser In The End ('Taylor)

Side Black: 1. 'Ogre Battle' (Mercury), 2. 'The Fairy Feller's Master-Stroke' (Mercury), 3. 'Nevermore' (Mercury), 4. 'The March Of The Black Queen' (Mercury), 5. 'Funny How Love Is' (Mercury), 6. 'Seven Seas Of Rhye' (Mercury)

The most immediately striking thing about *Queen II* is its grand and dramatic packaging. Freddie told Mick Rock to dream up a suitable record-cover design, and he came through with a stunning image based on a beautiful old George Hurrell photograph of movie star Marlene Dietrich. The front cover shows the band's starkly-lit faces against a black background. They all stare forbiddingly into the camera, Freddie bottom-centre with his arms folded and fingers splayed in a deliberate imitation of Dietrich's pose.

If the cover finally nailed the band's public image, the album itself saw them finally achieve some semblance of musical self-determination. The first thing to notice is the cavernous drum sound, which brings Roger centre-stage at last. Throughout the record, his tympani-like fills and flourishes are of a piece with the guitars' orchestral tones. Far more than on the first album, Roger's playing helps to shape the music.

*Queen II* was Brian and Freddie's first true moment of glory. May's guitar parts are marshalled into an overpowering, Hendrixian orchestra, with brutal riffs and meticulous leads all made to sound one-of-a-piece. Experimenting in parallel, Freddie contributes carefully-arranged vocal harmonies in huge abundance with nothing left to chance. The intricate harmonies took days and nights to lay down, with Freddie, Brian and Roger (John couldn't sing a note) overdubbing themselves hundreds of times – sometimes for a single phrase or word – until they sounded like some vast unearthly choir. The album didn't acquire the working title *Over the Top* by accident.

Unlike its patchwork predecessor, *Queen II* was also a concept album of sorts, with a mostly cohesive mood. It boasted a white and black side rather than the conventional side one and two. They decided to give Freddie the entire side black – the track-listing specifying it was to be listened to after side white which was composed by Brian except for one Roger song. The album's dual nature was perfectly expressed in the contrast between the gatefold cover's outer and inner band photographs– the latter showing them in stark white period costumes against a white background. Many of the lyrics play on themes of darkness and light, and a wintery mood pervades much of the music.

The LP opens with 'Procession': a sombre instrumental consisting of overdubbed, harmonised Red Specials. It sounds like electrified baroque music; the procession in question is possibly a regal one or perhaps even part of a funeral ceremony. Towards the end of this short passage, the melody morphs into that of the subsequent track 'Father To Son', which blasts off with a series of grandiloquent power chords. This song sets out the album's stall with its spacious production and self-conscious arrangement – an epic suggesting an Elizabethan rock band playing at some vast royal banquet. The lyric enacts a dying father's address to his son and heir, but the references to crowned kings and heroic battles place it in a mythologised past. The song gains an aura of pathos when it's remembered that Brian had a troubled relationship with his own father in the early-to-mid 1970s. Though Harold May had helped his son build a guitar, he disapproved of Brian's subsequent decision to pursue a career in rock 'n' roll rather than astronomy. It's possible the song's aching melancholy was Brian's attempt to make sense of their problematic relationship.

With 'White Queen (As It Began)', the aura of sadness continues, though Brian shifts gear into a more meditative mood. It's a wintry ballad, drawing on Celtic mythology via May's recent reading of the Robert Graves essay 'The White Goddess'. The lyric – which occasionally slips into the kind of Elizabethan English found in Shakespeare's sonnets – describes a mournful female deity who is finally revealed to be blind. Brian later admitted that the song was a heavily-coded paean to a girl he'd once fallen in love with at college but had been too shy to approach. As with several of his other early Queen songs, this one contains distinct, but related sections (Quiet and loud, basically); the elegiac verses are decorated with Roger's cymbal washes and Brian's delicate acoustic guitar. The louder sections come emblazoned with swelling banks of agonised guitars and ominous tom-tom rolls, with Freddie's impassioned vocals revealing the emotional gravitas that would soon become his calling card.

Brian's 'Some Day One Day' anticipates his later more-famous song ''39', being a softly delivered folk-rock number which features Brian on lead vocals for the first time on a Queen record. His fragile, enigmatic tone suits the song's sense of lovelorn mystery, with the lyric hinting at a traditional fairy-tale setting and casting the singer as a king addressing a suitor from his castle's misty battlements.

Side white ends on a rather incongruous note with Roger's truculent rocker, 'The Loser In The End'. The song rudely intrudes on the long fade-out from 'Some Day One Day', with Roger beating out a Bonham-esque introduction on drums and marimba. He sings it with his voice adorned by the same early rock-'n'-roll slap echo that featured on 'Modern Times Rock 'N' Roll' – the track attempting to strike a note of classic teenage rebellion. But with Roger stridently addressing 'mothers everywhere', and advising them to let their kids 'choose their own shoes', it doesn't exactly compete with The Who's 'My Generation'. 'The Loser In The End' isn't a bad song, but it feels out of place on the record, as if Brian and Freddie had forgotten to sit Roger down and explain to him what this album was all about. (Perhaps they had done so, and he simply hadn't listened!).

Side black opens with a mind-melting passage of tape-reversed guitar and gong before the onslaught of Freddie's 'Ogre Battle'. Progressive rock had always toyed with dark, Tolkien-inspired themes and characters, and here Mercury weighs in with an epic tale of monsters squaring up to each other within the hallucinogenic depths of a 'two-way mirror mountain'. Once again, the setting and action are redolent of childhood storybooks, with mysterious old men, absent pipers and dark-winged birds. Brian and Roger work together to create a ferocious setting of hammering drums and furious guitar riffs, after which the chorus breaks out into a piercing invitation to come watch the one-eyed, mighty-tongued, ocean-guzzling monsters battling each other at the end of the world.

'The Fairy Feller's Master-Stroke' arrives with some mischievous, prancing harpsichord: a prelude to one of Freddie's most fascinating early creations. Ever the art lover, he'd taken his fellow band members and Roy Thomas Baker to the Tate Gallery to see Richard Dadd's The Fairy Feller's Masterstroke – a painting the 19th-century artist conceived and executed in 1843 after murdering his father, believing him to be Satan in disguise. The minutely-detailed scene of bizarre human (and possibly not-so-human) characters offered a glimpse into Dadd's troubled mind. They also seemed to mirror the vast imaginative dreamscapes that Freddie and Brian were creating in Queen's music. Wanting to convey something of the strangeness of Dadd's vision, Freddie filled the song with archaic words and phrases from a poem the artist wrote to accompany his painting.

Musically, the song is busy and playful, with melodic sections that evoke half-remembered playground songs. The mid-point instrumental section, featuring some hair-raising Taylor falsetto, sounds like a demented pastiche of some old Hollywood movie score.

A musical segue takes us into Freddie's dreamlike interlude 'Nevermore': the first of two tracks produced by Robin Cable. The cascading piano accompaniment – recorded with Trident's distinctive reverb – is an uncanny portent of future Mercury songs: particularly of 'Love Of My Life' from the following year. The lyric, too, sees Freddie pressing pause on the fantasy themes and hyperbolic language to craft a heartfelt love song which some listeners have claimed (with no corroboration from Freddie) was a tribute to his lover Mary Austin.

The curtain is then pulled back on the album's spectacular centrepiece. Freddie's 'The March Of The Black Queen' is an almost grotesquely convoluted composition and arrangement, which pushed Trident's recording facilities – and Roy Thomas Baker – to their limit. Yet again, the song is a whirlwind of fantasy elements dominated by an all-powerful, elemental entity – in this case, the Black Queen, who is both 'lord of all darkness' and 'queen of the night'. This being's androgynous nature has led some listeners to suppose it was a projection of Freddie's personality or even a personification of his fast-developing powers as a singer, composer and rock-'n'-roll frontman. The song smashes together many different styles of music, from rock opera to prog to heavy metal, but with playful snatches of old-time jazz and even music hall. Buried within its dizzying structure are fragments of melody and arrangement ideas that were to rear their heads in later Queen songs – in particular, the subtle piano and guitar interplay which found its ultimate expression in 'Bohemian Rhapsody'.

If 'The Loser In The End' was side white's *sore-thumb* moment, the corresponding side black song is Freddie's 'Funny How Love Is'. The short, anthemic folk-rock ditty is a minor bauble in Mercury's cave of delights, though it's not without a certain innocent charm. However, Robin Cable's Spector-ish production results in a track that sounds like it's from a different album altogether (and possibly by a different band).

The album climaxes with 'Seven Seas Of Rhye', which segues out into the popular British music hall song 'I Do Like To Be Beside The Seaside', sung by the band and a few close friends (to the accompaniment of a Dubreq stylophone played by Baker) in a drunken fashion. It's a comical, surreal moment given the preceding track's darkly-magical nature, and it points towards the group's exploration of lighter material from the next album onwards.

If Queen had laboured under any illusions that their music would be understood and appreciated by the glitterati of rock journalism, the *Queen II* reviews brought them rudely down to earth. *Record Mirror*'s now infamous phrase 'the dregs of glam rock' was the most coruscating description meted out by a UK journalist. Canada's *Winnipeg Free Press* also put the boot in, dismissing the record as 'depressing', before going on to claim that 'The music sounds as if it was shoved into a computer and regurgitated in the form of a bunch of tired, unoriginal musical clichés'. *Rolling Stone* was equally hostile, citing, 'the lyrically muddled fairy-tale world (with) none of Genesis' wit or sophistication'.

From this point onwards, Queen and the music press developed a mutual antagonism that lasted many years. The bigger the group became, the more hatred they seemed to generate. Asked about it by *Circus* magazine in 1978, Brian meted out the response that was to become standard for all the group members: 'So many people in the press hate us because we've sidestepped them and got where we have, without them'.

By the time *Queen II* was released, the band had already begun a UK tour. Having previously worn stage clothes made by his friend Wendy Edmonds, Freddie now enlisted the services of fashion designer Zandra Rhodes, who'd also produced outfits for Marc Bolan. EMI A&R director Bob Mercer was horrified to discover that the new costumes – which Freddie insisted were for the whole band – were to cost £5000. Inspired by the work of fashion icon Tina Chow, Rhodes had previously come up with a wedding dress concept that she now chopped in half to create a distinctive cream-satin costume for Freddie. Featuring voluminous wing-like sleeves, the tunic allowed him to flounce and flutter about the stage like a huge eagle. Brian was fitted out with a similar outfit in black satin – more bat than eagle – though he, too, was later to wear a light-coloured version.

With their new outfits giving them an even-more-flamboyant image, Queen hit the UK concert circuit on 1 March with a gig at Blackpool Winter Gardens. The tour lasted until 2 April, attracting fervent audiences who'd bought into the mystique and mystery of the new album and its attendant hit single. Supporting Queen was the Liverpool band Nutz, whose just-released debut album had been produced by John Anthony. The shows introduced an important new element into Queen's live performance, with Freddie for the first time performing a song at the piano ('White Queen (As It Began)'). Not shying away from playing their more-ambitious creations, the band threw in 'The Fairy Feller's Master-Stroke', along with familiar crowd-pleasers including 'Liar' (now extended to a ten-minute epic), 'Great King Rat' and – of course – 'Seven Seas Of Rhye'.

But the tour wasn't without its problems. During the Aylesbury show on 2 March, Brian's post-inoculation troubles flared up again, and his arm became painfully swollen. After the gig, he received medical attention and was horrified to discover that a small segment of his flesh had become gangrenous. The condition was treatable, but it left him badly shaken.

Repeated power failures blighted the Glasgow show a couple of weeks later, causing the lighting crew to quit in disgust. At Stirling the next night, the show climaxed with the musicians cowering in a backstage kitchen while the audience rioted over the refusal to play a fourth encore. According to Roger, the 22 March show at The Paddocks on Canvey Island was the worst in the group's entire career, with Freddie forced to play his piano parts on the venue's old Wurlitzer organ. Though the great majority of the audiences were on Queen's side, trouble erupted in Manchester when the thrusting sexuality of Freddie's stage routine inspired one punter to shout, 'You fucking poof!' in a break between songs. Rather than ignore him, Freddie demanded that the house lights be turned on and the heckler identified, after which he was challenged to 'Say that again, darling!'.

Mercury was in his element when on stage, but friends and crew members later recalled him appearing stressed by the burgeoning pressure of fronting the band. It wasn't uncommon for him to throw up before a performance, and he was still struggling to pace himself. Despite these issues, the tour did contain some lighter moments – chief among them, Nutz singer Dave Lloyd's decision to run onstage naked during Queen's performance – the result of a bet with Roger, who'd promised Dave a bottle of champagne if he went through with it.

Though the music press didn't fall over themselves to cover the tour, there were a couple of notices. *NME*'s Julie Webb attended the Cambridge Corn Exchange gig on 9 March and was quick to point out 'the amazing amount of gear and a lighting system that Bowie would be proud of'. Noting that Mercury and Taylor were 'the genuine image makers in the band', she went on to describe Freddie slinking around the stage like 'a streetwalker whore tart'. Webb had picked up on Freddie's predilection for camp behaviour, and she became the first British writer to quiz him about his sexuality: 'Ask him if he's queer, and he'll turn around and say, 'I'm as gay as a daffodil, Dear'.

The tour was viewed as a success, with a sold-out performance at The Rainbow on 31 March allowing the band to feel like they'd *arrived*. The show was musically strong, and a decision was made to use a recording of it as the basis for a forthcoming live album. Music journalist Rosemary Horide – who'd given Queen a glowing review after an Imperial College gig – described the Rainbow performance as 'the conclusive evening for their reputation'.

Along with the plaudits, the tour paid off in record sales, with 'Seven Seas Of Rhye' and *Queen II* in April reaching numbers 10 and 5 in the singles and album charts, respectively. Even sales of the ignored debut album began to pick up: the record rising to a creditable 32 at the end of April. Sensing at last that Queen were on their way, John decided to abandon his masters degree. Brian, too – after much agonizing – told his PhD supervisor that he wasn't prepared to do any more work on his astronomy thesis. With Trident still holding onto the purse strings, the group remained flat-broke and with no clear idea of the future. But for better or worse, they'd finally committed 100% to a full-time career in rock 'n' roll.

# 1974 (Part Two) – Fuck it – A Hit's a Hit!

On 3 April, Queen trooped back into the BBC's Maida Vale studio to record another session for *Sounds of the Seventies*. Broadcast on 15 April, it was their most accomplished yet – the sound rich and cohesive, and the performances crackling with vitality. The version of 'White Queen' was particularly impressive, with Brian adding more elaborate guitar arpeggios and Freddie turning in a majestic piano solo. Roger's vocal on 'Modern Times Rock 'N' Roll' was far clearer than it had been on the recording, and he and Freddie added a dramatic call-and-response section towards the song's end.

*Queen II* was released in the States on 9 April. With the British tour having ended in Birmingham the week before, the band barely had time to catch their breath before commencing a major eight-week US tour on 16 April. For this jaunt, they again supported Mott the Hoople, despite the previous cake-based altercations. The itinerary started with a show at Denver's Regis College, where Freddie seemed nervous and out of sorts. In fact, throughout the tour, the enormity of performing in America (which British rock musicians so often viewed as the promised land) weighed so heavily on Mercury that he sometimes had to be cajoled into even getting out of the van. Despite his nerves, he usually delivered a powerful performance, though his flowing eagle-like costume and painted fingernails raised eyebrows among Mott's American audiences. Ian Hunter claimed that Freddie ended up stomping around hotel corridors in paroxysms of rage, demanding to know why the 'silly bastards' didn't accept his fairy-and-ogre-based epics.

Nevertheless, Queen found the tour as invaluable as the British leg had been, with the headliners' sense of *bonhomie* keeping them afloat. Roger told contactmusic.com in 2011: 'Mott were perfect for us. They had an open-minded, very rock-'n-roll, insane audience. They were liberated and colourful'. Brian agreed, claiming that Mott's antics helped coax him from his shell, transforming him from a studious astronomy postgraduate who played guitar, into a full-time partying rock-'n'-roller (At least occasionally!). The most dramatic instance of this occurred when they arrived in New Orleans on 21 April, and Brian enjoyed a brief romantic liaison with a girl known only as Peaches. She was to be somewhat enigmatically name-checked in one of his songs on the next album.

Despite the fun and games, the band didn't wallow in the lap of luxury for this first American tour. Shared and cramped hotel rooms were the order of the day, and it was often impossible to telephone home. They weren't showered with press accolades either, with most journalists writing about Mott and neglecting Queen. Even when they *did* get attention, it wasn't always positive – *New York Times*' John Rockwell mentioned Freddie's 'toothy, unconvincing posturings' and John and Brian's habit of 'standing around limply' in their corners of the stage.

On the last of six nights at New York's Uris Theater, Queen joined Mott for the final encore, singing backing vocals on a rousing version of 'All The Young Dudes'. They then boarded the bus to Boston for their date at the Orpheum Theatre. Brian had again been complaining about pains in his arm, but when he woke up in the Parker House hotel the next morning, he could barely move and knew something was terribly wrong. Stumbling into the bathroom, he saw his skin had turned yellow – a condition he immediately recognised as jaundice. It turned out that a combination of poor diet, tour stress and – crucially – the infected arm had left him with hepatitis. There was no choice but for Queen to cancel the remaining 18 tour dates and return home.

Many years later, Roger recalled the day in a Radio 1 interview: 'We were devastated. The tour had been cut short, so there were mixed feelings about that, but also we were very worried about Brian'. As the stricken guitarist was taking to his hospital bed in the UK, 'Seven Seas Of Rhye' was released as a single in the US. As if proof were needed that bad timing is anathema to rock-'n'-roll success, the record sank without trace. Perhaps the band found some solace in hearing that their US tour replacement – US group Kansas – were routinely facing boos and catcalls from disappointed Queen fans. The sense of gloom deepened when Brian's doctors told him there was no way he'd be well enough for a return to the States in autumn. That planned run of September dates was kicked into touch until the new year. Plans to release the live album – to which Brian was supposed to be adding guitar overdubs – were shelved.

With Brian marooned in hospital, the rest of Queen (with Baker and Mike Stone) regrouped and began writing and rehearsing material for a third album. Work initially took place in July at Rockfield Studios, amidst the beautiful scenery of Wales' Wye Valley. Situated just outside the village of Monmouth, Rockfield was one of the world's first residential recording facilities, its two studio spaces – The Coach House and The Quadrangle – housed in a pair of converted, old, solid-stone farm buildings. With clucking chickens scratching about in the yard, Freddie, John and Roger commenced backing tracks for Roger's 'Tenement

Funster', a Deacon number called 'Misfire' (his first for a Queen album) and a trio of Freddie songs: 'Flick Of The Wrist', 'In The Lap Of The Gods' and 'In The Lap Of The Gods... Revisited'. Given Brian's absence, it's ironic that the depleted band chose to work on two tracks destined to be dominated by his tempestuous playing: 'Brighton Rock' and the furious proto-thrash juggernaut 'Stone Cold Crazy'. This song had deep roots in Queen mythology, having been the first one they ever played in public – at their inaugural Truro concert on 27 June 1970. Created long before the group decision to always award songwriting credit to whoever cooked up the original idea, the track was eventually credited to all four members.

By the end of July, backing tracks existed for ten of the album's 13 songs, which now awaited vocal and guitar overdubs. Meanwhile, Brian had tried to keep busy while convalescing. From his hospital bed, he dreamed up a moody song called 'She Makes Me', along with the short-and-sweet lullaby 'Dear Friends'. He later recalled being racked with anxiety that the group were poised to replace him. His worries were compounded when – having finally met up with the band at Rockfield – he collapsed and had to be rushed into hospital yet again, this time with a duodenal ulcer.

The second recording phase took place at both Air and Wessex studios in August. Having recovered from his many ailments, Brian felt a surge of excitement when presented with the completed backing tracks. The following year he told *Circus Raves* magazine: 'When I came back, I was able to look at Queen as if I were an outsider. I'd never realized what it sounded like or how much the group had to offer. They'd got so much done without me – they were really good about it. All I had to do was go in and put my bits on'.

By the end of August, the album was mostly wrapped-up, though Brian managed to sneak in the new song 'Now I'm Here' at the last minute. This heavy and uncharacteristically raunchy number was his attempt to counterbalance some of the LP's more-whimsical Freddie moments.

Brian later revealed that he initially nursed doubts about one song in particular – ironically, the one EMI earmarked as a single. 'Killer Queen' – which Freddie later revealed he casually wrote 'one Saturday night' – was a sprightly pop track featuring jaunty and slightly off-key *jangle piano* (a Trident studio instrument with thumbtack-muted hammers) and extra-creamy, phased vocal harmonies. The lyric told the story of (in Freddie's words) 'a high-class call girl' whose pussycat playfulness disguised a heart of pure steel. The lyrics were colourful and ingenious, with references to 18th-century French queen Marie Antoinette and luxury French winemakers Moët et Chandon – both sounding like the most natural subject matter for a pop song. The subtle arrangement was enhanced by Roger's military press snare rolls and John's nimble bass runs. But ironically, it was Brian's velvety guitar harmonies that gave the track its luxurious sound. His contribution went well beyond guitar playing. Upon leaving hospital and hearing the song in progress, he had reservations about the chorus vocal harmonies and insisted on re-recording them. Despite his heavy input, he remained concerned that 'Killer Queen' was too lightweight for a single. However, following the song's release on 11 October (UK) and 21 October (US), radio stations spotted its commercial appeal and put it in heavy rotation.

Bolstered by a now-legendary *Top of the Pops* appearance in which Freddie loomed in front of the camera wrapped in a fur blouson, wagging a black-varnished fingernail, 'Killer Queen' began its inexorable rise up the UK singles chart, peaking at number two (later 12 in America) on 16 November, holding that position for two weeks. Far more than 'Seven Seas Of Rhye', the new single blasted a Queen-shaped hole into the record-buying public's consciousness. It also saw the band finally shake off accusations of being Led Zeppelin imitators. 'It was the turning point', Brian later acknowledged in an MTV interview – dismissing his earlier misgivings with the bullish remark, 'Fuck it, a hit's a hit!'.

With a huge hit single in their pockets, the band braced themselves for a long-delayed deluge of royalties. Still on their weekly £20-per-week salaries, they had for some time been griping at Norman Sheffield that their pay wasn't in step with their growing fame and acclaim. From Sheffield's perspective, he'd already spent a huge amount to get Queen where they were, including vast sums on equipment and publicity. Though the band's records were now selling in significant quantities, much of the money made so far had already been absorbed by Trident's exorbitant costs. According to Norman, there was more cash working its way through the tortuous twists and turns of the Trident/EMI publishing deal. But as Queen prepared for the release of their all-important third album, their frustration was mounting.

They were able to let off some steam on 16 October with yet another BBC session. Broadcast on 4 November – four days before the release of *Sheer Heart Attack* – this session focussed on material from the new album. This time, all four songs as broadcast were the LP's instrumental backing tracks, with Freddie singing live. If nothing else, the session is interesting for allowing us to hear 'Flick Of The Wrist' and 'Tenement Funster' as distinct, separate songs with their own endings, rather than being woven together as they are on the record.

### Sheer Heart Attack (1974)

Personnel:

Roger Taylor: drums, vocals, percussion, screams

Freddie Mercury: vocals, piano, jangle piano, vocal extravaganzas

John Deacon: bass, double bass, acoustic guitar, almost all guitars on 'Misfire'

Brian May: guitars, vocals, piano, genuine George Formby ukulele-banjo, guitar orchestrations

Producers: Roy Thomas Baker, Queen

Studios: Rockfield, Wales, July 1974; Wessex Sound, London, August 1974; Air, London, August 1974; Trident, London, August 1974 (Mixing)

Release dates: UK: 8 November 1974, US: 12 November 1974

Chart places: UK: 2, US: 12

Running time: 36:64

Side One: 1. 'Brighton Rock' (May), 2. 'Killer Queen' (Mercury), 3. 'Tenement Funster' (Taylor), 4. 'Flick Of The Wrist' (Mercury), 5. 'Lily Of The Valley' (Mercury), 6. 'Now I'm Here' (May)

Side Two: 1. 'In The Lap Of The Gods' (Mercury), 2. 'Stone Cold Crazy' (Queen), 3. 'Dear Friends' (May), 4. 'Misfire' (Deacon), 5. 'Bring Back That Leroy Brown' (Mercury), 6. 'She Makes Me (Stormtrooper In Stilettoes)' (May), 7. 'In The Lap Of The Gods... Revisited' (Mercury)

Given that Queen had most definitely *not* finished creating grand and regal rock albums, *Sheer Heart Attack* is a curious stylistic catalogue tangent. It's clear from Mick Rock's cover photo that the decision was made to present the band in a rather different light to the moody austerity of *Queen II*. Freddie said the group wanted to appear as desert-island castaways, so Rock had them sprawl in a circle on the floor – Freddie and Brian upright to the camera, with John and Roger upside down. Mick then shot the photos from the top of a stepladder. To suggest the idea of shipwreck survivors, he plastered them in Vaseline and turned a fine-spray hose on them just prior to obtaining the shot. The photo was rendered in rich, oily colours, which seemed to accentuate the oozing sexuality of the musicians' glistening bare chests, to say nothing of the thick black hair protruding from the opening of Freddie's unfastened trousers. Roger's long blonde locks were shown tumbling down towards the bottom of the image, an artificial effect courtesy of superimposed hair extensions. If the drummer had resembled a haughty young prince on the cover of *Queen II*, he now looked like a pouting soft-porn star. The back cover had an identical shot, but with vicious knife slashes intruding on the image. Instead of the usual ornate Queen logo, the band name – and album title – appeared in bold, block lettering in lurid red.

Just as the jacket design suggested Queen had come down to earth, the music on the LP offered a bracing alternative to its predecessor's grandiloquence. There were no black or white sides and precious-few magical characters and fantasy settings. But that's not to say the band had abandoned their love of experimentation. If anything, the album pushed the stylistic boat out much further than anything they'd attempted before. However, this time they'd made a conscious decision to create a sense of space within the music, presenting their more-outlandish ideas one at a time, rather than thrusting them at the listener simultaneously.

As if to stress that Queen had moved away from the land of mist-wreathed fairy tales, the opening Brian song 'Brighton Rock' was presaged with the sound of jaunty fairground music and a crowd: taken from the Elektra album *Authentic Sound Effects Volume 1*. Following a crossfade into fidgety guitar riffing, the band launch into one of their most iconic hard-rock performances in a song with musical roots stretching all the way back to the Smile song 'Blag'. Originally titled 'Happy Little Fuck', 'Brighton Rock' tells the story of a romance between two young lovers, set among the penny arcades and bustling crowds of the seaside town Brighton. Freddie adopts different vocal registers – including a dazzling falsetto – to depict the couple, Jenny and Jimmy. The lyric is a fervent dialogue between them, the old-fashioned syntax suggesting the story is taking place in Victorian times. As dramatic as it is, the vocal section is just a prelude to an extended Red Special workout, during which Brian uses an Echoplex to create overlapping, repeated guitar figures stretching to infinity. The solo would become a concert mainstay, invariably used as a platform for even-more-elaborate guitar pyrotechnics.

After 'Killer Queen' has provided some jaunty relief, Roger's 'Tenement Funster' begins an interlinked sequence of songs forming a kind of mini rock symphony much in the spirit of side two of The Beatles'

*Abbey Road*. Once again focusing on the joy and perils of a rock-'n'-roll adolescence, an echo-laden Roger sings to the accompaniment of a lone guitar, with bass and drums falling in behind him with menacing precision. Taylor had grown up in middle-class comfort in Truro, but his years of living in squalid student flats made him well-placed to narrate the story of a tower-block playboy whose financial hardship makes him dream of escape. Brian's guitar recreation of a revving car engine anticipates Roger's more-explicit ode to the joys of automobile ownership on the subsequent LP.

There was possibly some intended irony in the segue of 'Tenement Funster' into 'Flick Of The Wrist' – the former song about pretending to live the rock-'n'-roll dream, and the latter a bitter diatribe against the cutthroat realities of the music business. On the previous album, Freddie had written about duelling ogres, but here the violent imagery is all connected to being ripped off and ill-treated by obnoxious managers and ruthless executives. It's no coincidence that Mercury was embittered at still not possessing the riches to go with all his fame and success, and his anger spills over into 'Flick Of The Wrist'. The track showed Freddie and Brian working in almost-uncanny symbiosis, with the doom-like guitar riffs underscoring the lyric's venom.

The three-part suite concludes with Freddie's 'Lily Of The Valley'. A gentle piano reverie overlain with sensuous vocal harmonies, it finds him back amidst the fairy-tale imagery that had until recently been his calling card. It even references the messenger 'from Seven Seas', possibly the only time Freddie ever quoted one of his songs within another. Brian later described the song as 'utterly heartfelt', interpreting it as his friend's veiled attempt at coming to terms with his bisexuality.

The precious atmosphere is banished by the arrival of Brian's 'Now I'm Here', ushered-in with multitracked Red Specials chugging on one chord. A fanfare of rampaging drum fills and power chords launches the song proper, taking very few bars to establish itself as one of Queen's most swaggering rockers. With its lyrical references to 'Mott' and 'Peaches' (Brian's mysterious New Orleans sweetheart), the track is May's attempt to make sense of the chaos and excitement of the truncated US tour. The song was destined to become a durable live favourite, achieving the distinction of staying in the setlist longer than any other song.

Side two blasts off with Freddie's 'In The Lap Of The Gods' – the introduction allowing Roger to show off his most spectacular banshee-like wailing. The song is steeped in mystery and grandeur; the title and

**Right:** An early band shot reveals that only Freddie has so far mastered the 'smouldering looks to camera' technique.

**Below:** The *Queen II* album cover is brought to life for the 'Bohemian Rhapsody' video. They will not let him go. *(Bruce Gowers/EMI)*

**Below:** Friends, bandmates and business partners – poised for a second decade of success.

見本盤

**Left:** *Gettin' Smile*. Destined to become a collectors' item, Smile's 1982-released EP offered pre-echoes of the classic Queen sound. *(Phonogram)*

price realised. Telephone enquiries to Porthleven 312.

**Fri., April 17th, & Sat., 18th**

Their last appearance in Cornwall before splitting up. Your final chance to see the incredible

**Smile**

More LIVE, Progressive Music every Friday at

**PJ's St. Clement St., Truro**
Telephone (blank)

(This concert is in place of Sour Milk Sea, as advertised last week.)

NEXT WEEK

**Mike Chapman & Band**

**Threemilestone Y.F.C.**

**Right:** A local press advert for Smile's final gig in 1970: Freddie's band Sour Milk Sea had previously cancelled.

**WANTED**

**MOTT the HOOPLE**

QUEEN

MEL BUSH PRESENTS
NOV. 12 Leeds Town Hall
NOV. 13 Blackburn King George's Hall
NOV. 15 Worcester Gaumont
NOV. 16 Lancaster University
NOV. 17 Liverpool Victoria
NOV. 18 Hanley Victoria
NOV. 19 Wolverhampton Civic
NOV. 20 Oxford New Theatre
NOV. 21 Preston Guildhall
NOV. 22 Newcastle City Hall
NOV. 23 Glasgow Apollo
NOV. 25 Edinburgh Caley Cinema
NOV. 26 Manchester Opera House
NOV. 27 Birmingham Town Hall
NOV. 28 Swansea Brangwyn Hall
NOV. 29 Bristol Colston Hall
NOV. 30 Bournemouth Winter Gardens
DEC. 1 Southend Kursaal
DEC. 2 Chatham Central Hall
DEC. 14 Hammersmith Odeon

**REWARD**

75mins of the best Rock & Roll music in the land

**Left:** Supporting Mott the Hoople on their 1973 UK tour proved a steep learning curve for Queen.

**Right:** *Queen*. The debut album, mercifully self-titled after the band toyed with calling it 'Dearie Me'. (EMI/Queen)

by
**MICHAEL BENTON**

# Standing up for the Queen

QUEEN'S Freddie Mercury: Britain's New York Dolls?

**Left:** A July 1973 edition of *Melody Maker* attempts to draw parallels between Queen and The New York Dolls.

FREDDIE MERCURY is liquid heaviness. His friend Brian is an absolute dear. They're a pair of Queens. But let me explain.

Freddie and Brian have an amazing band. With two of their friends Roger and Deacon they're busily putting glam-rock on a new level by simply adding guts. To look at, the boys are divine — especially young Freddie who looks every-inch a star. But a word of warning, don't try it on with any of these Queens: They are hard and tough and their music is expressed in a very masculine manner. Their stage act is busy and they flash about in two colours — black and white. Not outstandingly gay, I think you'll agree.

"The idea of Queen was conceived by me whilst I was studying at college," says Freddie.

"Brian who was also at college liked the idea and we joined forces. The very earliest traces of the band go back to a group called Smile who made a single which was released in the States.

"The group was plagued by bad luck and it eventually split up. Queen has been going for about three years now, but until recently we've not had a suitable outlet for our music. Trident took us on and our first album, which has been in the can for almost a year is being released through EMI, recalls Freddie.

Adds Queen's Brian: "From the beginning the group has kept its original concept. This album is a way of getting all our frustrations out of our system which have built up over the years. We were into glam-rock before groups like the Sweet and Bowie and we're worried now, because we might have come too late."

Besides vocalist Freddie and guitarist Brian May, Queen's other two members are Roger Taylor who drumming romps power into the band's songs and Deacon John who blasts away at his growling bass.

Brian May's guitar is made from wood plundered from a hundred-year-old fireplace. It sounds remarkable and allows Brian to form an excitingly solid foundation to Freddie's voice. Two perfect partners — but more rapiers than partners.

They are Britain's very own New York Dolls — but better.

The group's first break came when producers John Anthony and Roy Baker invited them to make some demos. They hawked their product around innumerable London record companies eventually ending-up with EMI.

As a live band they work hard to entertain in true showbiz fashion. At the moment they're not particularly well-known, but they're already attracting screamers.

Until recently the band have had to divide their attentions between studies and Queen, but as Freddie explained: "We've always wanted to be pop stars and the group used to come first. Now we're all qualified we can concentrate more on the band.

"We're confident people will take to us, because although the camp image has already been established by people like Bowie and Bolan, we are taking it to another level.

"The concept of Queen is to be regal and majestic. Glamour is a part of us and we want to be dandy. We want to shock and be outrageous instantly. We don't want people to have to think if they like us or not, but to formulate an opinion the moment they see us."

Brian and Freddie are the main songwriters, but they write individually. Mercury has a tendency to fantasise melodic and is more down to earth. Their first album, "Queen," is a series of amazingly different songs, from faster-than-fast rockers to soft ballads. Traces of Yes and Black Sabbath can also be found, but structurally it all seems to sound original.

A single, "Keep Yourself Alive," has also been released in hopes of giving the band some early chart success. Like the album, it's commercial in a progressive kind of way. Spaced between the chunky verses, the group have incorporated a drum solo (with effects) and a tastey guitar solo which has an interesting synthesizer effect. Brian insists he doesn't use one though.

"Singles are important to us and to have a hit now would really help the band. We've more to offer than bands like the Sweet. We're not just pop, because our music covers a wide area," says Freddie.

The group are currently preparing to start recording their next album which they say will have a theme of "good versus evil." They say it'll be much fresher than the first, because early frustrations have been expelled via the first album.

"We're worried that the name Queen will give people the wrong impression. We want to be a good British regal rock band and we'll stick to that way of thinking. Our music should override the image, because we'll concentrate on putting out a good product the whole time. Teenyboppers will probably like us and we might get a bit of a 'pop' tag, but it won't last.

"At the moment we're just interested in creating a reaction amongst those who come and see us."

**Left:** *Queen II*. The band's second LP was nicknamed 'The Kitchen Sink Album' by its co-producer Roy Thomas Baker. *(Mick Rock/EMI/Queen)*

**Right:** 1974, New Theatre, Oxford. With his Zandra Rhodes-designed eagle-sleeved tunic, Brian attempts to upstage his fashionable friend.

**Left:** Queen's photogenic qualities were spotted early on by publications such as *Disc* magazine in 1974.

**Right:** *Sheer Heart Attack.* Desert island castaways with hair extensions and busted zips well to the fore. *(Mick Rock/EMI/Queen)*

**Above:** Brian appears to have had a rare haircut prior to this centre spread in the pop magazine *Mates* in 1974.

**Left:** *A Night at the Opera.* The fourth album's lush white gatefold owed something to The Beatles' self-titled 1968 LP. *(EMI/Queen)*

**Right:** After Queen were forced to cancel dates due to Brian's illness, Kansas became headliners on the '74 US tour.

**Left:** The 'Bohemian Rhapsody' video from 1975. The innovative video effects by Bruce Gowers have now been viewed one billion times on YouTube.

**Right:** The stately rhythm section of Queen from the 'Bohemian Rhapsody' video.

**Left:** The former dental student Roger Meddows Taylor adopts a bohemian lifestyle.

**Right:** The astronomer with the homemade guitar.

**Left:** *A Day at the Races* was Queen's parting shot to the art-rock of the 1970s. *(EMI/Queen)*

**Right:** With 'Bohemian Rhapsody' gliding up the charts, Queen began playing bigger venues in the US in early 1976.

JANUARY 29 & 30
MUSIC HALL
AT 8 P.M.
TICKETS
$7.50, 6.50, 5.50

QUEEN
special guest stars
Cate Bros.

TOMORROW NIGHT
Daydream Prod:
In Association W
JOHN REID ENTERPRI
Presents
IN CONCERT

Queen
Very Special Guest
CHEAP TRICK
FRI., JAN. 14—7:30 P.M.
General Admission—Festival Seating
$7.00 Advance $8.00 Concert Day
Tickets Still Available At Coliseum Ticket Center. Ticket Center Open Today 9 A.M. to 9 P.M.
MASTER CHARGE AND BANKAMERICARD WELCOME AT COLISEUM TICKET CENTER
DANE COUNTY MEMORIAL COLISEUM

**Left:** For Queen in the mid-seventies, 'tomorrow night' usually meant yet another concert.

**Right:** *Queen's First E.P* receives a self-explanatory title. *(EMI/Queen)*

**Left:** *News of the World.* Brian May always insisted that Frank was a gentle robot, but the jury remains out. *(Frank Kelly Freas, EMI/Queen)*

**Right:** A picture-sleeve edition of the single of 'We Will Rock You' released in France. *(Frank Kelly Freas, EMI/Queen)*

**Left:** 1977. Not always on the same page musically, Brian May and John Deacon learned to work around each other's differences.

**Right:** 1977. Former Kensington Market traders, now champions of the world. Roger and Freddie during an interview for *The Old Grey Whistle Test*.

**Left:** 1977. Freddie ponders another fascinating question during the same interview.

# Queen's Forum fare: Smoke but no fire

### By JUAN RODRIGUEZ
### for The Gazette

Played within the cavernous echo chamber of the Forum, the music of Queen sounds mainly like it's being played inside a tin can.

The patented harmonies were audible in last night's concert, yet the boom of the bass, beyond all proportions, and the general lack of clarity between each musical part, contributed to a sound no better than the loudest, crudest heavy metal rock group.

In fact Queen's sound was even more offensive because the group has been hyped as something more dynamic. One sensed that the only way their "music" is to be performed night after night is by sheer memorization. The changes of tempo are so quick and so facile. There was nothing there but mundane technique, the kind that can be rehearsed and repeated ad nauseum.

Freddie Mercury, earlier suffering from throat troubles, must've had a good rest in his hotel room, because he jumped about his microphone stand like a jackrabbit. Queen is propelled by the sound of its own success. Thus there is flashing, blinking lighting, phoney smoke and all the easily purchased gimmicks one comes to except from a "glitter-rock" ensemble.

When Brian May takes a guitar solo, it's as if he has distilled and concentrated past rock clichés. You've heard it all before, but not so short and automatic.

Audiences are baited to be carried away by the clockwork energy of performance which is why it hardly matters whether Queen turns it on or not

And that's why earlier in the day the clatch of teenaged fans admirers and groupies — pens and paper in hand, posing as the press maintained an hour-long vigil in the lobby of radio station CHOM for this latest rock phenomenon from Britain.

Queen was scheduled to appear for the obligatory ritual radio interview prior to the show

Last night's stand at the Forum was the 11th stop on a 40-city North-American tour which will end in mid-March in Alberta.

Naturally, the group got stuck at the airport, on the highway and in the hotel, so they were an hour late for the interview and, what was worse as far as the teen press was concerned, lead vocalist Freddie Mercury was absent, taking care of that tender throat.

Fortunately, Brian May, "the second most important guy in the group" according to the local promo man, arrived with drummer Roger Taylor The two have been in Queen a mite longer than the beleaguered Freddie

Queen employs tricky vocalese, changing tempi and tones continually, to provide a kinetic rush of excitement while actually telling a story, as in their mini-opera Bohemian Rhapsody, which soared to the top of the hit parade

A follow-up to their No 1 album, A Night At the Opera, has just been released to coincide with the tour it is appropriately called A Day At the Races

All sound and no substance, says Gazette reviewer Juan Rodriguez of Queen. From left: Roger Taylor, Freddie Mercuery, Brian May, John Deacon.

**Above:** Press hostility was something the band learned to live with throughout the 1970s.

**Left:** The popular magazine Look-in featured Queen on its cover at the start of the band's 'ground-zero' year of 1977.

**Left:** *Jazz.* The troubled seventh album, with keen cyclists tastefully on display. *(EMI/ Queen)*

**Left:** Freddie does 'The Fonz' on the set of the 'Crazy Little Thing Called Love' video in 1979.

**Right:** Famous for his drumming, it's sometimes forgotten what a massive contribution Roger made to Queen's vocals.

**Left:** Brian swaps his Red Special for a Fender Telecaster in the video of 'Crazy Little Thing Called Love'.

**Right:** John's shorn-headed look at the close of the seventies would later be replaced by a distinctly eighties-looking haircut.

**Right:** The UK's other royal family takes a turn around the Garden in 1978.

**Left:** A German magazine places Freddie's 'unitard' outfit front-and-centre, and shows him relaxing at home with his gold discs.

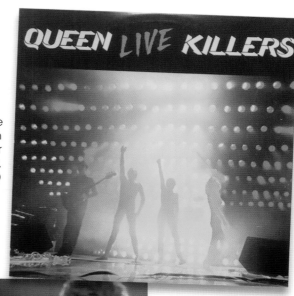

**Right:** *Live Killers*. After five years of dithering, Queen finally weighed in with their live magnum opus in 1979. *(EMI/Queen)*

**Left:** Brian faces the fans at the Hammersmith Apollo during one of the 'Concerts For The People Of Kampuchea' in December, 1979.

**Right:** Roger pours his heart and soul into singing about his car.

**Right:** 'Don't Stop Me Now' was performed by Queen for the last time ever at the end of 1979.

**Above:** Easy Deacon sports a fashionable slim-jim tie at Hammersmith Apollo.

**Right:** A December 1979 edition of *Melody Maker* gets the scoop on Queen's Crazy Tour.

QUEEN on stage (left); MAY tunes up (far right); MERCURY in full cry (bottom right)

# A Queen for the people

Queen want to be a people's band. They're fed up with the big halls and the ticket queues and feel the need for change. STEVE GETT corners Brian May.

QUEEN had just left the stage and returned to their dressing room, having played the opening date of their latest British tour. Fans were being ushered out of the massive hall at Birmingham's National Exhibition Centre, some being allowed to linger. Backstage, the atmosphere was calm and relaxed following the excitement generated by the band over the previous two hours. The only movement came from the occasional roadie seen silently scurrying back and forth to collect equipment.

chorus borrowed from Homer's 'Iliad'. Mercury's lead vocal is artificially pitch-bent, while the choruses are thick with lavish vocal harmonies. Roger's reverberated shrieks ride atop like the call of some ravished fairy-tale princess. Though fabulous and exotic, the song sputters out before quite reaching its potential. Much like the debut album's 'My Fairy King', this piece sounds like part of an imaginary concept album that Freddie had cooked up in his head but never succeeded in making a reality.

The listener is then thrust into the brutal urban surrealism of 'Stone Cold Crazy'. The song's roots lay in Freddie's Ibex/Wreckage days, and Queen had been kicking it around in rehearsals and live gigs from the beginning. The track alternates between passages of thrashing guitars and quick-fire vocal sections in which Mercury takes on the guise of an unhinged loner. The bizarreness of the song is matched by its raw power – machine-gun kick-drum beats and furious buzzing riffs which are a clear precursor to 1980s thrash metal.

The mood changes again with the arrival of 'Dear Friends' – the short lullaby Brian wrote in his hospital bed following the Mott tour's premature end. Though not explicitly referencing the anxiety he felt about his illness, the lyric reveals his fragile emotional state. The arrangement shows admirable restraint (unlike Def Leppard, who many years later turned in an ill-judged hard-rock version), with Brian's simple piano part complementing Freddie's yearning vocal.

From there, it's another left-turn into 'Misfire': the first Queen song credited to John Deacon. The bassist had decided not to let his vocal shortcomings get in the way of writing for the band ('I can't sing a single note', he later confessed), though it took him until the third album to come up with something worthy of inclusion. As would happen many times subsequently, John had taken his basic idea to the others for help in hammering out an arrangement and proper vocal melody. The song was originally titled 'Banana Blues' because of its summery feel and Latin sound. With typical panache, Taylor spices up the arrangement with flashes of cowbell and an exuberant tattoo played on an Italian Meazzi tom-tom. The lyric is playful and full of explicit sexual innuendo (not territory Queen had ventured into before), revealing John's love of black music.

*Sheer Heart Attack* is the first Queen album to include a novelty song – Freddie's joyous and camp 'Bring Back That Leroy Brown' summoning the ghost of ragtime. It's likely he'd been inspired by Jim Croce's recent hit 'Bad, Bad Leroy Brown': the story of a dandified gangster from Chicago's

South Side. Freddie's lyric is drenched in popular American slang and syntax, while some of the themes (people being shot, sent to jail, etc.) mirror the Croce piece. May's deft jazz stylings sprinkle fairy dust on what's already a tight rhythm section performance. Deacon is in top form on double bass for one break, and Freddie plays the jangle piano. As a bonus, Brian draws on his childhood music lessons by using a banjolele (as popularised by George Formby) as his main rhythm instrument.

The album's penultimate song is Brian's wistful 'She Makes Me (Stormtrooper In Stilettoes)': written while he was in hospital. A folk-tinged love song, it's wrapped in atmospheric reverb, and propelled by a slow, throbbing drum track. The ominous percussion led Roger to suggest the 'Stormtrooper In Stilettoes' subtitle, which adds an extra layer of mystery to an already enigmatic lyric. Sung by Brian in a quavering voice, it finds him supine in his lover's 'cocoon', unable to imagine who he'll be when he emerges. The track ends in a blur of disturbing sound effects, including stormy tom rolls, a wailing siren (the third side-two track to contain police references) and feverish heavy breathing.

The album climaxes with Freddie's 'In The Lap Of The Gods… Revisited'. It's a stately piano ballad in 6/8 time, with a vocal performance dripping in sadness. This time the 'lap of the gods' is a metaphor for a forsaken world, the disenchanted lover realising that the object of his affection is only after his money. Being a Freddie song, the hero's emotional pangs are blown up to epic proportions, with an endlessly-repeated chorus chant building with intensity as multitracked voices are added. With Freddie, Brian and Roger transformed into a vast, vengeful choir, the song finally has nowhere else to go and implodes into a blaze of doomsday static in the moments before the stylus reaches the run-out groove.

Almost five decades after its release, *Sheer Heart Attack* is often viewed as a seminal Queen album, and an early career milestone. As usual, though, contemporaneous reviews were mixed. In the UK, the *NME* proclaimed the record 'a feast. No duffers, and four songs ('Killer Queen', 'Flick Of The Wrist', 'Now I'm Here' and 'In The Lap Of The Gods… Revisited') that will just run and run'. The American magazine *Phonograph* took the opposite view, citing the band's 'apparent phobic dread of ever overdubbing fewer than 35 guitar parts on any song'. A review in *The Associated Press* predicted that Queen would be playing Madison Square Garden as headliners following the release of their next album.

The final two months of 1974 were spent on a whirlwind tour of
Europe, beginning on 30 October at Manchester's Palace Theatre. With
hot chart action from the new single and (from mid-November onwards)
the new album, the band's shows were greeted with hysterical fervour.
Riots broke out at three UK concerts – in Glasgow, Freddie was dragged
by his scarf into the audience. Fans rushed the stage in Leeds and
Liverpool, forcing the band to stop playing while Mercury attempted to
calm the crowd. Brian told *Record Mirror*: 'Most of the gigs in the north
were staggering: places like Bradford and Sheffield. They knew all the
songs – even the words on the new album, before it was out'.

*Sheer Heart Attack* was released on 8 November, quickly rising to
number 2, and only kept from the top spot by *Elton John's Greatest Hits*.
Acknowledging their recent musical evolution, Queen restructured their
setlist by injecting a large amount of material from the new album. For
the first time, they also put together a quick-fire medley which crammed
several song fragments into one extended piece and allowed the
musicians to demonstrate their virtuosity.

For the encore, the fans were treated to riotous versions of 'Big
Spender', 'Modern Times Rock 'N' Roll' and 'Jailhouse Rock', after which
the crowds were serenaded – via backing tape – to an instrumental
version of the British national anthem 'God Save The Queen'. The
majestic melody was rendered in the unmistakable multitracked tones of
Brian's Red Special and was punctuated by Roger's military snare rolls,
crashing cymbals and bombastic tympani. Recorded at Trident on 27
October, they got the idea for the track on the *Queen II* tour when fans
would sing the anthem while waiting for the group to take to the stage.
Though they hadn't yet hit on the idea of playing the tape as part of
their closing curtain call (the music having started a minute after they'd
left the stage and serenaded the fans as they filed towards the exits), it
became the climax to all their shows from this point forwards.

On 19 and 20 November, Queen returned to the Rainbow Theatre for
two sold-out shows. A film crew was present, capturing the band at the
height of their early pomp and splendour. Keen as ever to highlight
their mystique and glamour, Norman Sheffield made sure the cameras
were on hand to film the group's arrival at the venue: swishing from a
stretch limo up to the doors. In 2014, the Rainbow performances (along
with the sold-out March 1974 concert there) were finally released as an
official live album – *Queen Live at The Rainbow* – and today, make for
fascinating listening. What's immediately striking is the grandeur of the

*Queen II* material, which is taken at a slower tempo than on the record. In contrast, tracks from the debut album are attacked with gusto and a much wilder rock-'n'-roll feel, as are the scattering of songs from the new album.

The film of the Rainbow concert eventually saw cinematic release in highly-edited form – its 30-minute length ensuring it would never graduate from B-movie status. (It opened for Led Zeppelin's *The Song Remains the Same* in 1976, and *Jaws II* in 1978!) The show is visually compelling – the band emerging like rock gods from enormous clouds of dry ice. Freddie struts and preens, at one point brandishing a taloned glove which he tells the audience are a 'gift from Beelzebub himself'. Roger is flamboyance personified at the rear of the stage, his drums exploding in huge sprays of liquid – the result of them being soaked in beer prior to the performance. Yet, for all the music's epic grandeur, the high-octane audience interaction which would come to define Queen concerts is absent. Freddie speaks quietly and politely to the crowd between songs, his northwest London accent much broader than it would be in later years. For all the exotic finery of his new theatrical incarnation, there are still distinct flashes of the former graphic-design student Freddie Bulsara.

Queen ended 1974 with a short European tour, but it was not an auspicious climax to the year. The support band were southern-US rockers Lynyrd Skynyrd, who didn't respond well to Queen's fondness for eagle-themed outfits and eyeliner. Roger later dismissed that band as 'southern rednecks' – doubtless riled by the dirty tactics of Skynyrd's record company MCA who routinely planted audience members holding up placards saying 'Queen Suck'. Logistical problems also blighted the tour, with Queen's equipment truck ploughing into a railway bridge in Sweden, spilling all their equipment across the highway. After arriving late for a ferry crossing, they missed one concert entirely.

Despite the upturn in their fortunes over the previous few months, the group members went into the new year flat-broke and still at loggerheads with Trident over money and management issues. But 1975 was to bring momentous changes. Little could they have dreamed that by the end of the year, rock superstardom would be theirs for the taking. But the intervening months would be no bed of roses and no pleasure cruise.

# 1975 – Galileo!

Queen's first release of 1975 was the single 'Now I'm Here' in the UK on 17 January, backed with the highly-contrasting 'Lily Of The Valley'. It rose to a creditable 11 – not spectacular compared to 'Killer Queen', but evidence that the group's harder-rocking material had commercial potential.

The next day, John Deacon married his long-term partner Veronica Tetzlaff, who was already pregnant with their first child. Prior to the big day, John had approached Norman Sheffield, asking him to foot the bill for a new house: a request the Trident boss turned down flat. John wasn't the only Queen member to face refusal – at around the same time, Roger asked for a new car, and Freddie a grand piano. Both were refused. This was the cause of huge frustration and anger now that the band were successful pop stars, with a hit album on both sides of the Atlantic. They felt this was difficult to square with their measly salaries and down-at-heel lifestyles. Brian was fed up with living in a damp single room with no natural daylight, and Freddie's pride was injured at having to rely on Mary Austin's salary from the fashion store Biba, and a modest Kensington apartment giving them only a modicum of comfort.

Predictably, Sheffield had a very different take on all this. According to him, the band was still in debt to Trident to the tune of thousands – much of this the result of the company's purchase of a vast lighting rig for Queen's exclusive use. The recent American tour had also cost a lot, thanks to the cancelling of so many dates due to Brian's illness. Sheffield claimed the group had amassed considerable royalties by the end of 1974, but these couldn't be paid until the books had been carefully balanced. Unfortunately, the band's patience was exhausted. Having shared their woes with EMI's A&R director Bob Mercer, they were put in touch with lawyer Jim Beach who agreed to begin scrutinising their Trident contract for any potential get-out clauses.

With these business problems hanging over their heads, the band began rehearsing for a major US tour. The itinerary was onerous – beginning in Columbus on 5 February, and ending in Seattle on 6 April. Perhaps the tour's sheer scale was a reaction to the cool reception Queen had received in Europe at the end of 1974. So the group turned their backs on their homeland for the next two years and focussed on achieving that most-elusive but highly prized of all rock 'n' roll grails: the conquering of America.

The North American tour consisted of 38 shows in 30 venues and a mountain of promotional activity – including (much to their horror) at least two radio interviews in each city. Heavy schedules were common for British bands touring the States in the mid-1970s (Queen's main prog-pop rivals Electric Light Orchestra were also driving themselves into the ground in America in this period), but Queen's appetite for backbreaking graft knew no bounds. Asked many years later why he thought Queen had been more successful than most other British bands, Roger quipped with a great deal of truth: 'We worked a lot harder than most of them'.

One of the tour's support acts was Kansas – the group who'd attempted to fill Queen's shoes on the previous Mott tour. Kansas lead vocalist Steve Walsh later told classicbands.com that he'd found Queen to be 'nice people, except Freddie'. His view of Mercury was in line with that of Norman Sheffield – namely that Freddie was a vain prima donna who'd grown too big for his boots. Though there's enough anecdotal evidence to back this up, a more-charitable view would be that Freddie's bad behaviour was exacerbated by sheer work pressure. This was doubtless compounded by his obsessive perfectionism – anyone listening to mid-1970s Queen concert bootlegs will hear that attention to detail coming through in every note Freddie sang. Working flat-out like this over many weeks and months, it was perhaps inevitable he'd throw the occasional hissy fit.

It was also inevitable that his health would suffer. On the tour's second leg, Freddie began to lose his voice, and following the second of two Philadelphia shows, was diagnosed with throat nodules. When a consultant told him he shouldn't sing for the next two months, Mercury was distraught, and decided not to tell his bandmates. Somehow he got through the subsequent show in Washington, but it soon became clear that several dates would need to be cancelled. Two further consultants produced a less-ominous diagnosis, and after a period of rest, Freddie was able to resume the tour.

Audience reaction was feverish. Support bands Kansas and Argent both experienced the brunt of this; both were impatiently booed off stage on more than one occasion. Brian discussed Queen's rapturous reception in Cleveland and Detroit with New York's *Rock Scene* magazine: 'I felt they understood every note. It was incredible'. Press reaction was rather-more-mixed, with journalists sniffy about the band's overt theatricality. In particular, the prodigious use of dry ice was seen as ridiculous – a symptom of Queen's upstart determination to be viewed as rock legends before their time had arrived.

The band partied hard on the road, Roger later confessing that the daily rounds of radio interviews weren't made easier by his many appalling hangovers. They also found time to kick back as gig-goers, trooping *en masse* to catch Led Zeppelin's performance at the vast (and, of course, sold-out) L.A. Forum on 27 March. Despite words of reassurance from Jack Nelson, Brian glumly contemplated the unlikelihood of Queen ever managing to fill such a prestigious venue.

Remarkably, the musicians were given only a couple of weeks' rest and rehabilitation after completing the US adventure. Beginning on 19 April, a short tour of Japan saw Queen being treated like the rock royalty they'd always aspired to be. The itinerary began with a sold-out show at Tokyo's 10,000-capacity Budokan Hall, which was famous for having hosted The Beatles on their 1966 tour. In an uncanny imitation of the Liverpudlians' 1964 arrival in America, Queen's touchdown at Japan's Haneda Airport was greeted by thousands of screaming fans, after which the four dazed musicians faced the cameras at a rapturously-received press conference where they were presented with awards for high sales of *Sheer Heart Attack*. The opening concert was a near-riot, with Freddie forced to pause the music after fans rushed the stage, despite the best efforts of the venue's sumo wrestlers as security. The delirious crowd showered the band with gifts as they played.

Between shows, each Queen member was offered the protection of a personal bodyguard and were each also presented with an elegantly-flowing kimono. The four young men looked happy but slightly overwhelmed as they were filmed sipping Japanese tea, waited on hand-and-foot by deferential geishas. 'I think we're gonna move to Japan', Brian quipped as his turn came for a close-up. Freddie thanked the 'boys and girls' for an 'amazing welcome', his toothy smile as coy as ever. Over the coming days, he threw himself into Japanese cultural life, spending a fortune on clothes, porcelain, trinkets and titbits – burrowing as deeply as ever into his Trident expenses account. For all of Queen, the first tour of Japan was immensely important in terms of building up their self-esteem and confidence. For Freddie, it was also the beginning of a lifelong love affair with the country.

All euphoric experiences tend to be followed by a comedown. For Queen, the morning after the month in Japan was crushing, as they returned to the grey skies of England and their ongoing business troubles. They'd now decided that whatever happened with the Trident publishing and recording contracts (Jim Beach was still trying to free them of those), they no longer wanted to be managed by Jack Nelson. On the American tour, they'd made tentative approaches to legendary rock impresario Don Arden: head of Jet records, and Mafioso-like manager of ELO and Black Sabbath. As a result of the approach, Arden paid a visit to Norman Sheffield in England, and tried to bully him into releasing Queen from Trident. In the end, the band decided that their interests wouldn't be best-served by signing with Arden, who'd been known to have people dangled from sixth-floor office windows when they got on the wrong side of him.

Now back in London, Queen continued to network, speaking to high-profile managers like Harvey Lisberg, Peter Rudge, and the biggest beast of them all: Led Zeppelin's Peter Grant. However, they eventually decided to sign with Elton John's manager John Reid – a close friend of Freddie – who advised them to take time off from the road and focus on making the best album of their career.

Jim Beach's efforts were to pay off by the end of the year, with Queen finally becoming free of all Trident tentacles before the release of the next album. Queen would now be signed directly to EMI and Elektra. But this freedom didn't come cheap – the band agreed to pay a lump-sum severance of £100,000. In effect, this meant parting with all their long-delayed royalties at the very moment they were released from Trident. Sheffield insisted on retaining a one per cent financial stake in the band's next six albums. Having bankrolled Queen's success thus far, he was far from happy at the desertion of his main star clients. And unbeknownst to him, more bad blood would be spilt before year's end.

## *A Night at the Opera (1975)*

Personnel:
Freddie Mercury: vocals, vocals, Bechstein debauchery and more vocals
Brian May: guitars and orchestral backdrops
Roger Taylor: percussion
John Deacon: electric bass
Producers: Roy Thomas Baker, Queen
Studios: Rockfield, Wales, August-September 1975; Sarm East, Scorpio, Lansdowne, Roundhouse, London, September-November 1975
Release dates: UK: 21 November 1975, US: 2 December 1975
Chart places: UK: 1, US: 4

Running time: 43:17
Side One: 1. 'Death On Two Legs (Dedicated to…)' (Mercury), 2. 'Lazing
On A Sunday Afternoon' (Mercury), 3. 'I'm In Love With My Car' (Taylor),
4. 'You're My Best Friend' (Deacon), 5. ''39' (May), 6. 'Sweet Lady' (May),
7. 'Seaside Rendezvous' (Mercury)
Side Two: 1. 'The Prophet's Song' (May), 2. 'Love Of My Life' (Mercury),
3. 'Good Company' (May), 4. 'Bohemian Rhapsody' (Mercury), 5. 'God
Save The Queen' (trad. arr. May)

The concept of a make-or-break album often looms large in rock
biographies, and can sometimes be taken with a pinch of salt. However,
for Queen, it's no exaggeration to say their fourth album saved their
career. It was clear to them that their only path to salvation lay in
making a game-changer of an LP. Brian told BBC Radio 2 in 1999: 'We
had a kind of desperation about us at this point, as we were totally
bankrupt'. May said that if *A Night at the Opera* hadn't been a success,
'We would've disappeared under the ocean someplace'.

Roger later recalled driving through the countryside to the first
recording session – a tape of *Sheer Heart Attack* blaring and his heart
filling with trepidation about the task that lay ahead. To make matters
more nerve-wracking, the band was going into the new project with
hardly any pre-written material. Prior to commencing sessions at
Rockfield in August, they'd convened for three weeks of initial writing
and rehearsing at a country cottage called Penrhos Court in rural
Herefordshire. The house's owner Joan Murray had advertised it as a
practice space, though given she'd specified that hard rock bands need
not apply, Queen were lucky to secure it. (As an interesting aside, Joan's
daughter Tiffany later wrote a memoir called *Diamond Star Halo*, in
which she shared her fly-on-the-wall memories of Queen at work and
play in her family home.)

Queen didn't tend to jam material into existence. Instead, they'd
splinter off and work ideas up separately before bringing them back into
the rehearsal room. The hard-nosed process of choosing which material
to work on was painful, as some ideas were welcomed enthusiastically
while others got binned. For Roger and John – who were nowhere near
as prolific as Freddie and Brian – the stakes were much higher. As the
songs took shape, furious arguments could break out as a song's initial
writer fought to retain creative control. During the fourth album sessions
(as was increasingly the case as the years wore on), some of this tension

was dispersed by the band members spending long hours in separate studios – a working method identical to that favoured by The Beatles for the recording of their eclectic *White* album.

By now, each musician's personality – and the dynamic between them – was well-established. Freddie's fiery nature was, of course, a given. As the quietest member, John was nevertheless a strong-willed individual who (he later joked) 'shouted the most quietly' to get his way. Though Roger was the fun-loving, rock-'n'-roll animal of the group, he could be hot-tempered. Brian was slow-working and indecisive, yet also remarkably stubborn once he'd made his mind up about something. He was also a melancholy soul who was easily depressed by arguments and conflict.

Though the band bickered, the fiercest conflicts were between Brian and Roger. They'd known each other the longest, and often behaved like squabbling brothers. Despite all their differences, each band member shared an almost compulsive perfectionism. Music journalist Rosie Horide visited the group during the recording sessions, and later recalled: 'One day I spent with them, I don't think they did more than 30 seconds of music which actually got onto the record'.

Queen's search for perfection did indeed reach new heights on the fourth album. The basic facts speak for themselves. The band used five different studios (often simultaneously), and reportedly spent somewhere in the region of £40,000: money they didn't yet have. The recording took four months, with an enormous number of guitar and vocal overdubs piled onto the songs. If *Sheer Heart Attack* had seen the group trying to streamline their sound, the new work represented a return to the thinking process behind *Queen II*, while adding an extra layer of ambition. This time, they were not so much trying to equal *Sgt. Peppers*, as smash it out of the ballpark. They again had the help of the redoubtable Roy Thomas Baker, who'd now also parted with Trident and signed as a client of John Reid. Mike Stone – whose engineering skills had become indispensable – was also on board. The men's technical gifts would be stretched to the limit by the album's dizzying array of styles and moods – all of which had to be delivered with the utmost precision.

The record starts in eerie, dream-like twilight with a whirling passage of solo piano playing from Freddie. The prelude to his song 'Death On Two Legs (Dedicated to…)' is a fine example of the 'Bechstein debauchery' credited to him in the liner notes. His florid arpeggios conjure the romanticism of Liszt and Rachmaninoff, while hinting at a gothic darkness reminiscent of old horror movies. Following some foreboding guitar chords from Brian and piercing screams from Roger, a more-staccato piano passage rings out, after which the song lurches menacingly into its main theme.

The lyric is a sustained, corrosive portrayal of a bloodsucking, lawbreaking 'shark' who has purloined all the singer's money, and has now come back for more. This unnamed individual is a 'leech', 'killjoy' and 'bad guy'; worse – a 'sewer rat' intent on sucking his victim dry. The singer lobs his tormenter a series of sneering questions, asking him if he feels good, and daring him to a confrontation. Of course, in Freddie's mind, the villain of the piece was Norman Sheffield – the man who had (according to Mercury) enriched himself at the band's expense. Freddie's vocal tone is more aggressive than anything he'd so far committed to tape, though the overlapping phrases are reminiscent of the verses in 'Keep Yourself Alive'. As an album opener, 'Death On Two Legs' brashly sets out the group's store, announcing a newly-perfected brand of operatic rock 'n' roll. The song featured in the band's concerts over the next few years. Before the year's end, it also – perhaps inevitably – reignited legal hostilities with Sheffield, resulting in a costly libel lawsuit.

A hard edit yanks the listener into the following song. Freddie's joyous 'Lazing On A Sunday Afternoon' exists in a very different musical universe, its central character a loveable dilettante whose suburban surroundings and day job don't prevent him from fulfilling all of his heart's desires. The title and lyric are a nod to The Kinks' 'Sunny Afternoon' (which contains the phrase 'Lazing on a sunny afternoon'), though the central character enjoys happier circumstances than Ray Davies' bankrupt millionaire. Freddie sings in a clipped, camp and very English style, which encourages us to picture him parading around the streets of 'London town' in the costume of a young English gentleman from a P. G. Wodehouse comic caper.

Roger had also become adept at crafting songs which reflected – or possibly even poked fun at – certain aspects of his own character. 'I'm In Love With My Car' was the most succinct example to date. From 1976 onwards, at least one of Roger's old Truro friends noticed that whenever he came home to visit his parents, a bigger and flasher car would be parked outside the Taylors' quiet suburban home. Ironically though, when Roger wrote the song, he barely had enough money for the most clapped-out old motor. This didn't prevent him airing his passions, and in the song, he joyfully declares (with tongue firmly in cheek, we hope) that his dream machine means more to him than his lady. He also rhymes 'forget her' with 'carburettor', and sings of brandishing his 'grease gun' as a symbol of masculine virility. With its revving guitars and spluttering drum fills, the music pumps exhaust fumes from every oily orifice. Cheesy as hell and quite deliberately so, the song eventually earned Roger enough money to buy the car of his dreams.

The album shifts gear for John Deacon's 'You're My Best Friend' – an easy-on-the-ear pop song that's streets ahead of his 'Misfire' on the previous record. A devoted husband and soon-to-be father, John had decided that the band needed at least one song that expressed a man's love for his wife in the sweetest terms. The arrangement's defining ingredient is the Wurlitzer electric piano – an instrument that had graced Marvin Gaye's 'I Heard It Through The Grapevine'. Though Freddie was usually happy to back John up, his distaste for electric keyboards resulted here in a minor standoff, and John was left to play the catchy Wurlitzer part himself.

Queen's catalogue isn't exactly littered with acoustic folk tunes, but on the rare occasions they do pop up, they tend to be written by Brian. Sung by him in an appealing, fragile voice, ''39' has one of the album's most intriguing lyrics, being the story of a team of volunteer astronauts who return to Earth after a one-year intergalactic voyage, only to discover that on Earth, a century has passed. May wrote the song in the early hours of the morning, having dreamed the concept after reading a short story by mystical German-Swiss writer Hermann Hesse. Giving vent to his passion for astrophysics, Brian fashioned a time-travel fable exploring a similar 'lost in space' theme as David Bowie's 'Space Oddity'.

Musically, ''39' is a master class in taste and restraint, with meticulous acoustic guitars riding atop a softly throbbing bass drum and decorative tambourine. Roger shines with heavily-reverberated falsetto shrieks, and the soaring group harmonies are never far away.

Over Queen's career, it was usually Brian who made sure each record contained at least one genuinely raunchy rock track. On 'Sweet Lady', he achieves the ingenious trick of delivering a riff-heavy song in 3/4-time. No great shakes lyrically, it allows him to stretch out into heavy-metal territory and showcase the powerful synergy he'd always enjoyed with Roger. The closing accelerates into a manic double-time section – a favourite May/Taylor trick, and one they repeated on later tracks 'It's Late' and 'I Want It All'.

Side one closes with Freddie's 'Seaside Rendezvous' – another old-time music-hall-style number, joyfully evoking the ragtime of the interwar years. Freddie casts himself as the debonair, pleasure-seeking loverboy, and it's easy to imagine him roaring onto the promenade in his Edwardian Roadster, honking his horn at the girls and flashing his toothy grin. Freddie and Roger pull off the imitating of an entire brass section using just their voices. Roger also provides a short kazoo solo, and for an encore, performs a tap-dance with his fingers in thimbles on the mixing desk. With its jangling piano and nostalgic *bonhomie*, the song distilled that part of Freddie's psyche that was pure, unsullied British Empire – a world of cravat-sporting, teddy-bear-cuddling gentlemen leading lives of moneyed leisure.

Side two opens with Brian's 'The Prophet's Song', which, like ''39', was inspired by a dream – this time not about intergalactic adventure, but the breakdown of relationships on Earth. The recording makes use of atmospheric sound effects and exotic instrumentation – namely, a howling wind and a toy koto – a six-string guitar given to Brian by a fan on the Japanese tour. The track shows May at his most foreboding, with the Red Special played in drop-D tuning to evoke a Black Sabbath-like menace. The track would be monumental even if it just consisted of its verse and chorus segments, but it's expanded into truly epic proportions through the inclusion of a two-and-a-half minute *a cappella* vocal section in which a tape-delayed Mercury harmonizes with himself until the entire sound picture is saturated in overlapping Freddies.

Already masters of the ingenious segue, Queen surpass themselves with the delicately arranged bridging passage into the next track. 'Love Of My Life' is the first and greatest of all Freddie's heart-on-the-sleeve love songs. Its melody is achingly sad, and its lyric painfully up-front in expressing the singer's desolation at being forsaken by his lover. As lush vocal harmonies accompany him, it's clear the affair is already over and he's a broken man. Along with elegant, Chopin-like piano-playing and tasteful electric guitar, the track features Brian's valiant harp-playing. Through the years, Freddie was typically cagey about the lyric, and various competing theories have emerged regarding whether it was a message to Mary Austin, with whom he was still nominally in a romantic relationship. (Other sources suggest the song was a heavily-veiled depiction of Freddie's then-recent infatuation with a music executive called David Minns.)

Of all the album's songs, Brian's 'Good Company' is perhaps the most ingenious, given that its complex instrumental layers were largely all his work. In his youth, May had been a big fan of The Temperance Seven

– a British Dixieland jazz ensemble dedicated to playing the popular music of the interwar years. In typical mad-boffin fashion, Brian tried to recreate the group's vintage, swinging sound with his Red Special imitating all the woodwind and brass instruments. He also dug out the banjolele he'd used on 'Bring Back That Leroy Brown', to capture that authentic Dixie flavour. Sung by Brian, 'Good Company' is a series of reminiscences on the part of a lonely old man who's taken his father's advice to look out for his own interests rather too seriously. The song's bouncy feel and cheerful atmosphere (enhanced by a dazzling guitar orchestration) is in stark contrast to the story's downbeat denouement.

The album was to end with the majestic tones of Brian's arrangement of 'God Save The Queen', which itself climaxed with Roger's rolling tympani. But first, there was to be one more Freddie song – namely, the composition that was destined to elevate Queen to the status of rock gods. 'Bohemian Rhapsody' dated back to Chris Smith and Freddie's aborted late-1960s Imperial College songwriting sessions. Freddie had periodically tinkered with it over the years, more recently playing fragments of it for Roy Thomas Baker at the latter's house. Betraying its origins as one of Freddie Bulsara's earliest attempts at composition, 'Bo-Rhap' (as it was later nicknamed) contained several excerpts from a handful of never-completed songs. Having played a particular segment to Baker, Freddie grandly announced, 'This is where the opera section comes in!'. It was a clear signal that he'd now hatched a musical plan of Wagnerian proportions.

The story of this track's creation, in three different studios in summer 1975, has now passed into rock legend. Freddie arrived at Rockfield with the composition already scribbled in the pages of his father's old accounting notebooks. The recording of the various segments was painstaking, with Baker forced to leave 30-second gaps on the tape so that the mysterious joining sections (which only Freddie seemed to know the contents of) could be added later. When it came time to record the opera section, Freddie, Brian and Roger overdubbed so many vocals that, according to May's later testimony in a 1993 issue of *Guitar World*, the tape turned transparent. The choral vocals were repeatedly bounced down, baked-into the production long before Mercury recorded his lead vocal and allowed everyone to finally hear his grand design.

There was a feverish quality to Freddie's creativity – his fellow musicians watching, bemused as he repeatedly returned to the vocal booth to add yet more operatic phrases and flourishes. Mixing the track was a Herculean task, with one nearly-complete pass ruined (after many hours of aborted versions) by the studio owner's wife suddenly entering the room to present Freddie with a birthday cake.

The track begins with an *a cappella* vocal overture, before proceeding to a typically-melancholy Freddie piano/vocal section in which the protagonist confesses to having killed a man. The lyrics are addressed to his 'Mama' in the form of a tragic confession. Roger and John provide a steady rhythm while Brian's guitar soars and screeches in sympathetic counterpoint.

The third section is the opera, where the hero is put on trial and hounded by alarming, almost demonic voices. This segment is rife with literary, cultural, historic and religious references, including Scaramouche (a clown from the Italian *Commedia dell'arte*), Figaro (hero of operas by Mozart and Rossini), fandango (a traditional form of Spanish and Portuguese dance) and Beelzebub (a Hebrew deity later recast in Satanic guise by Christianity). The Italian astronomer Galileo is also mentioned (more than once!), along with the word 'bismillah' – a devotional phrase from the Qur'an; its presence marked the first time Freddie acknowledged his Islamic heritage in a song. The entire section is executed with immense flair and confidence, no doubt facilitated by the technical expertise of Roy Thomas Baker, who'd recorded Gilbert and Sullivan operas during his years as a studio apprentice.

The fourth section is a full-blown heavy-metal work-out, Brian's guitar rampaging while our tragic hero openly defies the forces ranged against him. Finally, there's a return to Freddie at the piano, his final despairing vocal phrases beautifully accompanied by gentle guitar lines, rounded-off with Roger's majestic gong strike.

In every sense, a *magnum opus*, 'Bohemian Rhapsody' (running time 5:53) managed to distil in one track what *Queen II* took an entire album to achieve, but here with added pop hooks to boot. The song dripped with grandeur and mystery and helped create the impression that Freddie was deeply versed in the mysteries of *serious* art music. Yet Freddie remained modest about his operatic knowledge, later telling *Rolling Stone*'s Steve Turner: 'I don't really know anything about opera myself, just certain pieces. I just wanted to create what I thought Queen could do. It's not authentic, and it's no sort of pinch out of *The Magic Flute*. It was as far as my limited capacity could take me'.

According to Brian, no one else in the band ever thought to ask Freddie what his most famous song was all about. This was, in fact, quite normal for Queen, whose members were too self-conscious to explain their lyrics to each other. Freddie himself often dismissed fan and critic attempts to interpret or project meaning onto 'Bohemian Rhapsody' – once telling British DJ Kenny Everett that the entire lyric was 'random rhyming nonsense'. Despite this brush-off, it's sometimes thought that the song was Mercury's attempt to portray the immense upheavals that were happening in his personal life – namely the battles he was having with himself over coming out as gay.

It's almost universally accepted that *A Night at the Opera* is Queen's definitive album. It's certainly their most complete musical statement, and a record that allowed them to bring to fruition the many different (and in some cases disparate) ideas they'd been playing with since their career began. From a performance perspective, it's their most incisive work, with all four musicians delivering creative and exciting parts which lock together in a manner entirely belying the fragmented nature of the recording process. The album's sound is meticulous and contoured, if not aggressively sculptured in places – sharpening all the edges that most post-1960s rock music had left warm and fuzzy. The vocals are startling, bold and original – the mass harmonies are not just an ornamental feature but an intrinsic part of the music's construction.

The compositions boldly go to new places. John takes his first major leap forward as a songwriter, while Freddie finds a way of joining the dots of the various progressive ideas he'd been tinkering with since 'My Fairy King'. Roger's drumming finds a fresh sense of scope and finesse, and Brian bolsters his reputation as an inventive technician who could – if he chose – record entire *orchestral* albums on his own using just his guitar.

The album's grand title was arrived at following a post-mixing social event at Roy Thomas Baker's home, where he treated the band to a viewing of the Marx Brothers' movie *A Night at the Opera*. An ornate cover design soon followed, with a white gatefold jacket displaying a beautiful, full-colour recreation of Freddie's crest emblem. The colour scheme and gatefold were suggestive touches, putting record buyers in mind of the Beatles' eponymous 1968 release, which (coincidentally?) also featured a dizzying melange of pop styles, including heavy rock, gentle ballads, early jazz and comedy. There was a further nod to that epochal album in the four small black-and-white photographs of Queen inside the cover. For the first time since the debut, they were posing casually, and looked (as The Beatles had) like regular Joes. Also, this was the first Queen album to boast a full-colour photographic inner sleeve – displaying on one side a set of individual shots of the musicians on stage. On the other side, they were pictured wreathed in their trademark billows of dry ice, this time looking like the major stars they were about to become.

Prior to the LP's release in November, the 'Bohemian Rhapsody' single was unveiled in the UK on 31 October. Freddie had pushed for the song's release but had, in turn, encountered significant pushback from EMI executives, who pointed out that a record longer than three and a half minutes would struggle to get airplay on British radio. There was even initial disquiet within the band, though they ultimately formed a united front in refusing to edit the song down. This confrontation between Queen and EMI now seems emblematic of the huge freedom and power enjoyed by successful 1970s rock bands, though it's remarkable to consider that Queen were at this point still at rock bottom financially and were hardly in a position to pull rank on their record company. Ironically, despite their apparent solidarity in the face of industry intransigence, the group argued over which song would go on the B-side. Baker later claimed that Roger locked himself in the tape closet at SARM studio, refusing to come out until everyone agreed that the lucky song should be his 'I'm In Love With My Car'.

EMI might've still refused to play ball had Roy not given maverick British DJ Kenny Everett (a friend of Freddie's) an advance copy of the single. Despite being told not to play it on his popular radio show, Everett proceeded to do so no fewer than 14 times in one weekend. By Monday, record shops were besieged with customers demanding a copy of the band's bizarre new record. EMI was forced to back down.

With the single selling at an astonishing rate, Queen hooked up with *Live at The Rainbow* director Bruce Gowers to film a promotional video. The resulting clip – filmed at Elstree Studios and costing nearly £4000 – found the band bringing to life Mick Rock's regal photographic portrait from the *Queen II* cover, minus the period dress (John is seen wearing a Queen t-shirt!). It was an inspired idea, catapulting the band's most iconic pose into millions of homes. Given that the record was to spend nine weeks at number one – its period of peak glory spanning Christmas and New Year – this meant a phenomenal amount of exposure.

'Bohemian Rhapsody' was destined to be revered as a true landmark studio recording, its musical brilliance and technical wizardry earning it a place in the history books alongside 10cc's 'I'm Not In Love' (itself a chart-topping 1975 record) and The Beatles' 'A Day In The Life'.

Put simply, had Queen split up in the first months of 1976, their first number-1 single (and its attendant video) would've still guaranteed them the kind of immortality granted only to the most select artists. The song earned its composer an Ivor Novello award, and sold over 1,000,000 copies in its first few months alone. In a matter of months, the single made Freddie and Roger (the composer of the B-side) extremely wealthy. From inauspicious beginnings banging around on a piano in an Imperial College music room, Freddie Bulsara had – just one year shy of his 30th birthday – entered the pantheon of legendary rock songwriters. And yet, in his own mind, he was just getting started.

Released on 21 November, *A Night at the Opera* earned mostly positive reviews. One or two critics cast a stern eye at the exorbitant recording costs *and* at certain self-aggrandizing statements from Freddie – he boasted to one bemused journalist that the LP included 'the finest songs ever written'! *Melody Maker* found a middle path, telling readers the record offered 'musical range, power and consistently-incisive lyrics', before archly adding, 'If you like good music and don't mind looking silly, play this album'. The group themselves seemed happy with the work, though Brian sounded surprisingly tentative when he told *Circus* magazine, 'We're searching for new directions, and most of them are sort of half-formed. We've got the *Queen II* feel in some places, and in others, we've got the *Sheer Heart Attack* polish. I don't think we're quite sure where we're going'.

Brian may not have been sure where his group was going, but for everyone else, their upwards trajectory was clear to see. Queen were already six shows into an ecstatically-received British tour by the time the album came out. And by the end of the month, 'Bohemian Rhapsody' had hit number 1. The run of dates was followed by a Christmas Eve concert at the Hammersmith Odeon, broadcast live on *The Old Grey Whistle Test*. Many years later, it was finally released on CD and DVD as *A Night at The Odeon: Hammersmith 1975* (2015), providing a crucial snapshot of the band as they sounded right on the cusp of their first wave of British superstardom.

*A Night at the Opera* hit number 1 on 27 December. It remained in the top 20 for the next 13 weeks, chalking up four of them in the top spot. The album also reached number 4 in the US, making the band a significant concert draw in North America. Not only had Queen arrived, but they were here to stay.

# 1976 – Grotesquery of the First Order

Queen achieved success in a notoriously flat period in British pop music. By the end of 1975, the glam scene had largely dissipated, and progressive rock had also worn a little thin. Most of the era's huge bands (Zeppelin, Pink Floyd, Yes, Sabbath) had already released their most groundbreaking or successful albums, and as the new year progressed, there was a creeping sense that pop and rock had entered the doldrums. As the year wore on, the grass-roots movement of pub rock increased in popularity – its dressed-down heroes embodying an approach that was the complete antithesis of Queen's. But though Eddie and The Hot Rods and Dr. Feelgood rejected prog's pomp and flamboyance, they also resisted the temptation to wind the musical clock back to 1968 and play endless guitar solos while staring at their shoes. Instead, they stepped on the gas and turned up the aggression, laying the groundwork for the punk rock that, from the middle of 1976, began to inject some much-needed excitement into British rock.

Queen were to deal with the punk fallout in their own good time, but that time would not be 1976. Instead, the year saw them add more sophisticated layers to their music. This condemned them to being viewed – in the UK at least – as an irrelevant anachronism before they'd even had a proper chance to taste their long-awaited success.

The band members still maintained a strong professional relationship. Not that there weren't any tensions – in fact, quite the opposite. Thanks to the runaway success of 'Bohemian Rhapsody', Freddie and Roger were finally about to become wealthy men. But Brian and John were yet to strike gold in the lucrative singles chart, and there was only an incremental improvement in their financial situation. Such obvious inequalities frequently tore other bands apart. But Queen had a collective eye on a more long-term concern – not just wealth and success, but the great music they still had it in them to create. This would be their first year of freedom from Trident's financial and managerial shackles, and a new sense of self-determination put a spring in their step.

The first Queen-related release of the year was a Freddie-produced single by singer-songwriter Eddie Howell. A former Parlophone recording artist, he was now signed to Warner Bros. and had released an album called *The Eddie Howell Gramophone Record*. The Freddie connection came about thanks to his romantic involvement with

Howell's manager David Minns, who'd introduced the two the previous autumn at the launch party for Howell's LP. Subsequently, 'Man From Manhattan' was recorded at Sarm East: the sessions slotted in around Queen's work on *A Night at the Opera*. The song was a sprightly affair, featuring Freddie on piano, Brian on guitar, and both providing distinctive Queen-style backing harmonies. The record was bright and worthy, picking up substantial airplay in early 1976 and leading to a re-release of Howell's album, now retitled *Man from Manhattan*. Unfortunately, a Musicians' Union dispute over the lack of a work permit for the American bassist who played on the single, resulted in the record being yanked from radio and banished from the charts. Despite this inauspicious end, Howell's song remained close to Freddie's heart, and Queen often performed it as part of their soundchecks.

Queen began their next US tour on 27 January, spending the best part of two months crisscrossing the country and enjoying the adoration of packed houses. When journalist Mitchell Cohen asked Freddie why Queen had captured the imagination of US record buyers in a way that T. Rex and Slade hadn't, he imperiously dismissed them as niche artists: 'I didn't think America would go for groups like that. I think they fall into a category that America wouldn't accept. We want to make sure we appeal to as wide a cross-section as possible; not just cater to a fragment of people. It's limitless – we want to hit everyone'.

Released as a single in the US on 2 December, 'Bohemian Rhapsody' was gliding up the charts on its way to an eventual peak position of 9. In the mid-1970s, the US was some way behind the UK in giving coverage to promotional clips of chart singles. This is perhaps why Queen's most famous song missed the top spot in America, though the extensive airplay it received guaranteed a tidal wave of publicity.

For this tour, the support acts were southern soul duo The Cate Brothers and Detroit meat-and-potatoes rockers Bob Seger and The Silver Bullet Band. The itinerary took in theatres, convention centres and smaller sports arenas in such cities as Boston, Philadelphia, Cleveland and Chicago. There was also a four-night residency at New York's Beacon Theatre. During the run of early-February dates, the band were happy to hook up with their old comrade and mentor Ian Hunter, who was in town recording his second solo album, *All American Alien Boy*. Freddie, Brian and Roger ended up singing backing vocals on the song 'You Nearly Did Me In', though their distinctive contribution didn't rescue the LP from chart oblivion.

Brian later recalled the tour as the first where sold-out houses became the norm. Speaking to a UK newspaper the following year, he paid tribute to American audiences who were – unlike their more-reserved British counterparts – 'ready to explode from the beginning'. No strangers to mini-riots and stage invasions, the group saw fan hysteria reach new levels in New York, where three female fans embarked on a vicious fight over Freddie's scarf while it was still around his neck. He was in full throttle throughout the tour, telling one journalist prior to going on stage that he intended to sing until his throat felt 'like a vulture's crotch'.

Away from the band, Freddie and photographer Mick Rock explored New York's gay nightlife, encountering iconic scene dwellers such as Glenn Hughes: moustachioed singer with the soon-to-be-huge disco act Village People (as opposed to the British singer and bassist who was in Deep Purple at the time). The group had provocatively modelled themselves on well-known American stereotypes, including the cop, cowboy and – in Hughes' case – the eternally leather-clad biker. Rock later recalled Mercury avidly watching Hughes dance on the bar at a gay hotspot called the Anvil Club, after which Freddie 'was never the same again'. Though Freddie didn't immediately rush out to buy his own leather outfit and peaked cap (or indeed resolve to grow his own horseshoe moustache), the idea for a radical image change was now planted in his mind.

Onstage and off, Queen continued to dazzle. In addition to multi-hued lighting and jets of dry ice, they now started using explosions and visual trickery to create a sense of shock and awe. During 'Now I'm Here', the crowd was treated to the bewildering sight of two Freddies (the doppelganger being Freddie's personal assistant Pete Brown), illuminated in separate spotlights on either side of the smoke-wreathed stage. The half-deafened-and-blinded fans loved it, but critics were divided about the music. Queen sounded 'hollow at the core' according to a correspondent from *The New York Times*, who also lambasted the group for being 'calculated and precious'. This was in stark contrast to *The Los Angeles Times*, which, after a performance at Santa Monica Civic Auditorium, announced, 'A major new force in rock has officially been crowned. The band's name – quite appropriately – was Queen'. The paper predicted that the next time the group returned to America, they'd be selling out 10,000-seat arenas.

Following the US tour, Queen took ten days off before plunging back into the live fray and returning to Japan. This visit was even more fevered than the first, with fan adoration reaching new heights. The itinerary was crushing, and saw the group in some cities playing two shows in one day. With his voice buckling under the pressure, Freddie indulged in some *rest and rehabilitation* courtesy of several hugely-self-indulgent spending sprees. He flashed his cash so much that fans coined the term 'crazy shopping' to describe his voracious appetite for jewellery, clothing, trinkets and electronic gadgets. Brian opted for a more-creative brand of therapy – inspired by the Japanese fans' adoration, he wrote a special song in their honour, titled 'Teo Torriatte' (Let Us Cling Together)'.

Next, the band jetted to Australia. While their previous jaunt there had been conducted under a cloud, this time they were embraced enthusiastically. There were more stage invasions and yet more peril for Freddie as he was leapt upon by excitable female fans. The singer had now taken to stripping down to a pair of red-and-white hotpants – one reviewer describing him sprinkling roses into the audience as the stage 'spewed blinding light, colour, sand, smoke and explosives'.

As usual, Mercury channelled every iota of energy into entertaining his *darlings*, but offstage his behaviour was becoming difficult. Prior to performing at Sydney's Hordern Pavilion on 17 April, he refused to walk the short distance to the venue, and insisted on being chauffeur-driven through a crowd of people. Somewhat predictably, the pedestrians began milling around the car and blocking its progress, with some people jeering at Freddie as he glared at them over the top of his champagne glass. According to road-crew chief Peter Hince, once safely in his dressing room, the singer took revenge for this inconvenience by breaking a small mirror over the head of Pete Brown before then ordering him to sweep up the glass. If Mercury was learning how to be a proper rock star, it seemed appropriate to do it in the style of an imperious royal mistreating his manservants.

With live work finally wrapping up towards the end of April, Queen took several weeks off, and EMI got on with releasing the band's next single. In view of the dramatic disparity in the band members' earnings, it was agreed that Brian (who'd recently married his long-term girlfriend Chrissie) and John (who'd become a father) should carve up the single between them. The A-side would be John's 'You're My Best Friend', with Brian's ''39' on the back. The strategy paid off when the single cracked the UK top 10 and the US top 20. As the sequel to 'Bohemian Rhapsody', 'You're My Best Friend' achieved the double trick of sustaining Queen's chart momentum while appealing to listeners who knew and cared little about progressive rock. The record's success was a personal triumph for John, given that it was only the second song he'd written for the group.

By the summer of 1976 – just as the first stirrings of punk were being felt in London – Queen were ready to begin writing and recording their new album. It would categorically *not* be a punk rock record. Having already scaled the heights (or, as some critics would have it, plumbed the depths) of big-budget multitracked grandiloquence and becoming a household name off the back of it, the band saw no immediate reason to tamper with the formula. But they *did* decide to assert their creative independence by producing themselves. Roy Thomas Baker – who'd helped guide and shape Queen's music since their earliest Trident sessions – took their decision in his stride. Having just signed a lucrative production deal with CBS, Roy now had a caseload of other artists to produce anyway, starting with Ian Hunter. Mike Stone, though, was to remain as one of the engineers for the new Queen album.

The band again used several recording facilities to create the new opus, with many sessions taking place at The Manor in Shipton-on-Cherwell, Oxfordshire. Owned by Virgin Records impresario Richard Branson, The Manor had been the location for the recording of Mike Oldfield's epochal *Tubular Bells* in 1972/1973. It was an eight-bedroom residential sprawl housing a billiard room, swimming pool, and tennis courts in the rambling grounds. The studio's luxurious control room was kitted out with state-of-the-art recording equipment.

The sessions saw the group tinkering with several ideas left over from *A Night at the Opera*. But from the start, the band envisaged a rather less-manicured sound, instructing Mike Stone to capture a more natural room ambience by moving the mics further away from the instruments. Though several songs had a more-loose feel than the previous LP, many of the arrangements were even *more* intricate than before, with dizzying arrays of instrumental overdubs and thickly-textured vocal harmonies.

The earlier summer sessions were productive but also stressful – the result of having no external producer to oversee the work. 'There were huge rows some days', engineer Gary Langan later revealed, singling out Freddie as throwing the fiercest tantrums of all. But the rest of the band weren't immune to stress either. In his later photographic memoir *Queen in 3-D*, Brian commented on why he began sporting uncharacteristic facial hair in 1976: 'The beard was a sign of me getting depressed. Making albums was quite a grim time for me because it was always a bit of a fight. We were all pulling in different directions'.

After several weeks of intense work, the band were desperate to let off steam, and in September were glad to play four shows. Two were warm-up theatre concerts at Edinburgh Playhouse; the other two were larger outdoor shows at Cardiff Castle and London's Hyde Park. In addition to providing some welcome respite for a group going mad with cabin fever, these dates assuaged their anxiety at having played no UK shows at all in 1976. The concerts also allowed them to test some of the new material – namely, Brian's new rocker 'Tie Your Mother Down', and Freddie's delicate torch ballad 'You Take My Breath Away': performed solo with Freddie at the piano.

Introduced by Freddie with the immortal words, 'Welcome to our picnic by The Serpentine', the 18 September Hyde Park concert became a true milestone in Queen's performing career, with more than 150,000 people in attendance and the band in top form. The date was no random choice, being the sixth anniversary of the death of Jimi Hendrix. Richard Branson envisaged the concert – which included support acts Kiki Dee and Steve Hillage – to be a sequel to Pink Floyd's legendary 1968 Hyde Park show and The Rolling Stones' similarly gargantuan 1969 event.

Resplendent in a white spandex unitard – a skin-tight chest-revealing costume reminiscent of those worn by ballet dancers – Freddie held the vast audience in the palm of his hand, much as he was to do at *Live Aid* nine years later. Though clock-watching police prevented the band from playing a much-deserved encore, the show was a huge buzz for all concerned. Brian later told *Eclipsed* magazine: 'It was one of the most important concerts in our career. It was wonderful to come back, see this crowd and feel this reaction'. The event was successful on a personal level for Roger also, thanks to his meeting Richard Branson's glamorous assistant Dominique Beyrand: Roger's soon-to-be girlfriend and eventual mother of his two children.

With the noise of the Hyde Park crowd still ringing in their ears, Queen returned to the studio, and finished recording in November. With director Bruce Gowers having helped make Queen four of the most recognisable faces on the planet thanks to his work on the 'Bohemian Rhapsody' video, he was again hired to film a promo clip for the new single: Freddie's gospel-pop epic 'Somebody To Love' (b/w Brian's heavy rocker 'White Man'). This time Gowers took a less melodramatic approach, interspersing footage of Freddie at the piano with a shot of the band gathered around a microphone, apparently laying down the song's complex barrage of harmonies. (The dead giveaway that they're just miming is the inclusion of John 'can't sing a note' Deacon!) The single – released on 12 November (10 December in the US) – gave the LP advance publicity. 'Somebody to Love' was an immediate success, rising up the UK chart to peak at number 2 (13 in the US).

## A Day at the Races (1976)

Personnel:
Freddie Mercury: vocal, piano, choir meister, tantrums
Brian May: guitars, vocals, Leader of the Orchestra
Roger Taylor: drums, vocal, percussion, pandemonium
John Deacon: Fender bass
Producer: Queen
Studios: The Manor, Oxfordshire, July 1976; Wessex Sound, London, October-November 1976; Sarm East, London, October-November 1976
Release dates: UK: 10 December 1976, US: 18 December 1976
Chart places: UK: 1, US: 5
Running time: 44:21
Side One: 1. 'Tie Your Mother Down' (May), 2. 'You Take My Breath Away' (Mercury), 3. 'Long Away' (May), 4. 'The Millionaire Waltz' (Mercury), 5. 'You and I' (Deacon)
Side Two: 1. 'Somebody To Love' (Mercury), 2. 'White Man' (May), 3. 'Good Old-Fashioned Lover Boy' (Mercury), 4. 'Drowse' (Taylor), 5. 'Teo Torriatte (Let Us Cling Together)' (May)

*A Day at the Races* came packaged in another lavish gatefold (this one black), with more ornate typography and another luxurious, full-colour version of Freddie's regal crest. The album once again borrowed the name of a Marx Brothers movie, cementing it in the minds of record buyers as an official sequel to *A Night at the Opera*. Brian once even claimed that he wished the two records had been released simultaneously, so similar were they in conception and presentation.

While it's undeniably true that *Opera* and *Races* share a certain opulence, the latter has a distinctive identity. Leaning more towards pop-rock than art rock, it's far more streamlined than *A Night at the Opera* and eschews that record's jarring segues and tangential juxtapositions. Instead, *Races* flows smoothly (perhaps – according to its critics – too smoothly), and its carefully-chosen motifs or musical signatures help to unify the listening experience. As a result, the record feels more mainstream than anything the band had released up to that point.

The LP opens with two ominous gong crashes, after which Brian enters with a massive orchestration of distant-sounding electric guitars playing a stately melody with an oriental flavour. The opening sequence – including the gong – is the first of the album's musical tributes to the band's legion of devoted Japanese fans. (Its ceremonial flavour also recalls Brian's earlier composition 'Procession' from *Queen II*.) The piece then morphs into an elegant tapestry of Red Specials. Inspired by the architecturally-impossible staircase drawings of M. C. Escher, Brian made use of the Shepard tone (its creator, American cognitive scientist Roger Shepard), superimposing guitar parts to create the illusion of an ever-ascending sequence which never actually goes anywhere.

Cutting razor-like through the atmosphere, Brian's 'Tie Your Mother Down' matches the hard-rocking power of the previous album's opener 'Death On Two Legs'. But unlike that song, it has a relentless groove and an infectious, bluesy sense of fun. The Rory Gallagher-inspired head-bobbing riff (Queen's first full-on shuffle) had been in existence for several years, Brian having written it on acoustic guitar while conducting his zodiacal light research in Tenerife at the start of the 1970s. He dreamed up the title and chorus at the same time, but it took Freddie to persuade him that the song wasn't unsuitable for Queen. The band gives a spirited performance which is more louche than any of their previous heavy tracks. In retrospect, it's clear the song blasted a whole new path for the band, allowing them to channel their harder-rocking instincts into more-commercial territory.

While a disorientating hard edit was used to conjoin the previous album's first two tracks, a respectful silence separates 'Tie Your Mother Down' from Freddie's 'You Take My Breath Away'. A delicate piano ballad inspired by his semi-illicit romance with David Minns, it was written in spring, after the Japan tour. The song – less openly sentimental than 'Love Of My Life' – is performed by Freddie, save for the mid-point entrance of delicate electric guitar harmonies. Mercury uses a soft, pure vocal tone, at times enveloped in creamy harmonies. His spare, romantic piano lines are performed with conspicuous *rubato*: a tempo-quickening-and-slowing technique often used in classical music.

Brian's 'Long Away' boasts an uncharacteristic jangly sound, having been recorded on a Burns 12-string guitar fitted with the same pickups favoured by Stratocaster players like The Shadows' Hank Marvin. Sung by Brian in his now trademark husky tone, it has a windswept sound befitting its lyric, which again finds its composer expressing loneliness and homesickness.

'The Millionaire Waltz' was inspired by Freddie's great admiration and affection for John Reid, whose canny managerial dealings had set Queen on the path to becoming millionaires before the decade's end. In addition to summoning the spirit of light opera composers Gilbert and Sullivan, the song was a nod of sorts to Johann Strauss II – the 19th-century Austrian composer of luxurious and light music, including operettas, ballets, and of course, waltzes. Perhaps his most famous composition was 'An Der Schönen Blauen Donau': 'The Blue Danube'. With its calculated air of refined gentility, that piece provided a touchstone for Freddie's musical antics on 'The Millionaire Waltz'. From John's high-precision bass filigrees to Freddie's bouts of Bechstein debauchery, the song oozes an almost defiant decadence. But it's also awash with mischief and humour – particularly the middle waltz section, where Freddie's polka piano and Brian's elegant guitars conjure the atmosphere of a Viennese ballroom. Just to be clever, the band also throws in a short heavy-metal passage.

The conspicuous piano presence gives side one a certain cohesion. There's yet more on John Deacon's 'You And I' – a driving power-pop song with a gutsy Freddie lead vocal, raucous electric guitars, and acoustic guitar played by its composer. That year, Freddie told DJ Kenny Everett: 'John's songs are good and getting better every time. I'm getting worried, actually'. Written in tribute to John's wife, 'You and I' indeed seems to show Deacon in competitive mood. Its accomplished melody bounces along with the effortless commerciality of a Paul McCartney chart-topper.

Side two opens with Freddie's landmark song 'Somebody To Love', which revealed his huge love and admiration for the gospel recordings of Aretha Franklin (he later said her *Amazing Grace* was his favourite album of all time). With its fervent lead vocal and stirring piano, the track has a church-like sound, with the same swinging 6/8 time-signature used on 'In the Lap of the Gods... Revisited' and later recycled for 'We Are The Champions'. The group's vocal harmonies are overdubbed into infinity – weaved into the arrangement as a call-and-response with Mercury's lead vocal. For all the track's bombast, the lyric speaks of loneliness and despair as the singer bemoans the daily grind of his loveless life.

Queen rarely strayed into political territory, but Brian's 'White Man' is notable for an angry lyric that skewers the 17th-century New World colonists who treated the Native Americans brutally. Freddie takes the lead vocal while Brian wraps his creation in rasping, bluesy guitar, with the Red Special in drop-D tuning as it had been for 'The Prophet's Song'. But unlike that track, 'White Man' lacks a certain epic quality, having a rather uninspired chorus and a plodding verse feel.

Mercury's 'Good Old-Fashioned Lover Boy' reboots the album's sense of fun and adventure, casting the singer in the role of a besotted lover pouring his amorous energies into a night on the town. The song dallies with vaudeville elements, though the sound is smoother and more refined than it had been on 'Seaside Rendezvous'. If anything, it's like a swish West End musical number, and it's easy to imagine Freddie cruising home from the Ritz restaurant, sipping Champagne in the back of a gleaming Mercedes and celebrating another successful evening of romancing.

Roger's sole contribution to the album gives the impression he's trying to move beyond the macho teen spirit of his usual output. 'Drowse' is a surprisingly lovely evocation of the lazy, hazy days of a misspent youth, with a double-tracked Taylor lead vocal that lacks his customary sardonic bite. The lyric depicts the drifting reflections of a small-town dreamer as he wafts through life worrying about getting old. Glistening with Brian's elegant slide-guitar work, it's one of Queen's mellowest songs and, for Taylor, something of a musical tangent. By the next album, he'd be back on more-familiar hell-raising territory.

The album concludes with Brian's 'Teo Torriatte (Let Us Cling Together)', written – as he put it in his book *Queen in 3-D*, 'about the strong bond we as Queen felt with the Japanese people'. It's a Freddie-sung ballad with the kind of anthemic chorus that was later to become the group's speciality in the 1980s stadium years. The lyric has an autumnal feel as the singer ruminates on mortality, while also taking comfort in a loving relationship that he hopes will survive the passing years and ultimately transcend death. The chorus is sung in Japanese – translated by the band's friend and interpreter, Chika Kujiraoka. Featuring Brian on acoustic piano, electric piano and harmonium, 'Teo Torriatte' culminates in yet more choral overdubs, before ending in a reprise of the opening track's endless climbing staircase of guitars. It's a grand and entirely-fitting finale to a record that would come to be viewed as Queen's parting shot at the ingenious art rock of the mid-1970s.

In the UK, no expense was spared in launching the album via a high-profile public appearance at Kempton Park Racecourse in Sunbury-On-Thames – where, happily, all four Queen members happened to bet on the winning horse. More good vibes came in their direction courtesy of a well-wishing telegram from Groucho Marx. The band lost no time in talking up their new creation in the music press, with Freddie telling *Circus* magazine, 'It's new and slightly different, but definitely still Queen'. He also admitted it had been 'difficult trying to maintain our usual idiom, and, at the same time, coming up with songs that are different and more interesting'.

Despite such valiant pre-emptive strikes, the British pop press was unsympathetic to the new LP. By the close of 1976, punk was gaining serious traction. By extension, the younger generation of musicians and music writers viewed art rock as irrelevant claptrap. Queen themselves might've thought their new music was 'different and interesting', but a song suite dripping with influences such as Chopin, Strauss and 1960s psychedelia was never going to curry much favour. 'I hate this album', wrote punk champion Nick Kent in *NME*, before describing the record as 'grotesquery of the first order'. *Sounds* agreed, claiming Queen were 'too formulated, too smart-ass, too reliant on trickery'.

While the critics sneered, record-buyers had other ideas. The album became Queen's second UK chart-topper and reached five in the US. But despite this commercial triumph, the press vitriol rankled the band. Having suffered criticism for being glam latecomers, they were now being accused of terminal irrelevance in the face of upstarts like the Sex Pistols. But ironically, the latter outfit had something to be grateful to Queen for. On 1 December, Freddie's dental appointment meant Queen had to pass up an opportunity to appear on *Today*: an early-evening British TV show with a large family audience. In Queen's absence, the obstreperous Pistols stepped in – guitarist Steve Jones outraging the show's middle-aged host Bill Grundy by calling him a 'dirty fucker' live on air. The incident caused huge controversy, making household names of the Pistols, and embedding punk rock in the hearts and minds of British music writers and record buyers. As 1977 dawned, it became clear that the old guard of high-gloss rock bands from the early-to-mid-1970s were confronting a stark choice: continue adding musical frills and be permanently consigned to rock's back pages, or get back to basics and win over a new, younger audience. For Queen of course, the choice was a no-brainer.

# 1977 – Ground Zero

1977 was the year Queen's career went into overdrive, with six months of touring and 100 shows played. Battle commenced in January with a three-month blitz of North America, which in some cities saw them gravitate to sizeable arenas. For a significant chunk of dates, they were supported by Irish rockers Thin Lizzy, who managed to straddle both hard rock and the emerging punk sensibility. Given that it was the Queen's Silver Jubilee year, Freddie made sure the package was publicised as The Queen Lizzy Tour: a title not exactly in tune with the iconoclastic spirit of the times.

With Thin Lizzy in fighting form, the stage seemed set for some fiery inter-band hostilities. But surprisingly, Lizzy's guitarist Scott Gorham later recalled Queen treating them with a degree of respect not always displayed by headliners of their stature. Of course, this didn't mean the music hacks could resist heaping praise on Lizzy's streetwise swagger while taking potshots at Queen. As the tour reached New York, Brian told *Melody Maker's* Harry Doherty: 'The local press has been almost unanimously anti-us – the fashionable, easy slagging-off that tends to happen a lot by local journalists who pick it up from the big guys. *They* want to be famous, too, so they go in and slag off the big band. I think it's all on a very childish level'.

As if challenging critics to poke fun, Queen piped elegant Chopin piano music over the PA in the gap after Lizzy's opening performance. Brian's Escher-inspired guitar fantasia opened each show, after which a volley of smoke bombs announced Freddie's entrance. Bounding on in a white *kung fu* outfit, he then slipped behind a speaker to emerge moments later resplendent in his chest-revealing white leotard. He was still fond of swishing around the stage in a kimono whenever the mood took him. But he was just as likely to parade around in a tiny pair of shorts while scattering the audience with carnations.

The setlist now took in several songs from *A Day at the Races*, with 'Somebody To Love' a particular challenge due to its many vocal harmonies. Remarkably, 'The Millionaire Waltz' was also attempted – the group determined to show that whatever fairy dust was scattered over their records, they could replicate the magic live. The one exception was the choral section of 'Bohemian Rhapsody', for which the band substituted a backing tape while they disappeared into the wings, emerging with renewed vigour to perform the heavy metal section at blistering volume.

The tour took place during a particularly cold North American winter. One date was cancelled due to a lack of heating: the result of a diesel tanker becoming stranded *en route* to the arena in Dayton, Ohio. In Chicago, Freddie caused an uproar when he refused to allow a queue of freezing fans into the venue until the band had completed a lengthy soundcheck. Brian took a hit for the singer later that evening, slipping over on stage after being attacked with a vengeful shower of eggs.

Queen partied hard on this tour, and an appetite for Bacchanalian excess began to emerge. Tales have circulated of marathon parties, at which topless waitresses dispensed limitless booze and exotic dancers performed eye-watering strip shows. Queen lore agrees that such goings-on had less to do with the shy and retiring John and Brian, and more to do with the band's rampant party animals, Freddie and Roger. Mercury, May and Taylor also began dining together in Romanic splendour after each concert, much to the bewilderment of road crew and security staff, who were accustomed to groups fleeing the scene as soon as they left the stage. Having brought his wife and child along on the tour, John made a habit of retiring early with a cup of cocoa.

While on this tour, Freddie called time on his relationship with David Minns and began courting young male fans and hangers-on. He remained close friends with Mary Austin (and indeed remained so for the rest of his life), but had pretty much turned his back on a heterosexual love life. He now threw himself into a gay lifestyle, his sexual appetites supercharged by his newfound liberation. With this freedom came a shift in his stage performances. All traces of the early, fey Freddie vanished, and a more thrusting physicality became evident. The vest and moustache were still three years away, but Mercury's transformation had begun.

With the band still on the road in March, EMI released 'Tie Your Mother Down' as a single, b/w John's 'You and I'. The A-side had become a live fan favourite, and remained so for the rest of Queen's career. The single, though, was a commercial disappointment – stalling at 31 in the UK and barely denting the US top 50. As the record was shipping to stores, Queen enjoyed the thrill of playing two sold-out shows at the prestigious L.A. Forum, where – two years before – Brian had gone green with envy at the sight of a packed house for Led Zeppelin. In between the two dates, Freddie, Brian and Roger squeezed in a visit to the home of Groucho Marx. They presented the legendary comedian with gold discs for sales of *A Night at the Opera* and *A Day at the Races*, and posed with him for what must've been one of Marx's last press photographs. He'd pass away that summer.

At the end of March, the jet-lagged Queen returned to the UK for a brief period of rest and relaxation. In their absence, the country had begun gearing up for the Silver Jubilee – an event capable of whipping a sizeable chunk of the population into a patriotic fervour while millions of others looked on with disdain.

By now, punk rock had colonised the London music scene, with The Sex Pistols preparing to release their bile-spewing anthem 'God Save The Queen'. Such filth and fury dismayed the royalty-loving Freddie, who'd persuaded his bandmates to donate the fee for a forthcoming London show to the Jubilee Fund. Though not enamoured with the hype surrounding punk, Roger enjoyed the musical ferocity and anti-establishment attitude of The Clash and The Damned. He also took an interest in parallel developments in the US, checking out edgy records by the likes of Talking Heads and Devo. Taylor would ensure that at least some of the punks' hard, stripped-back sound started filtering into Queen's music.

Before any thought could be given to the next album, there were more live commitments to be met. A two-month tour of Europe commenced in Sweden on 8 May, culminating in two shows at London's Earl's Court on 6 and 7 June. On tour, the band attended an EMI press reception in Rotterdam, where they were awarded no fewer than 38 silver, gold and platinum discs for record sales in Holland alone: a sure sign they were now big business on the continent.

The shows were as flamboyant as ever, with Freddie sporting a checkered leotard modelled on one worn by world-famous Russian ballet dancer Vaslav Nijinsky. This costume was to define Mercury's lithe, balletic 1977 image. Its intimations of high culture would also set him on a collision course with punk hell-raiser Sid Vicious, during sessions for the next Queen album.

For the band's final Earls Court appearances, they unveiled a fabulous new lighting rig known as The Crown, which rose into the air at the start of the show and descended at the end. (ELO's manager Don Arden later *borrowed* the gargantuan spectacle for that group's career-defining 1978 tour.) With the show's theatrical elements now in overdrive, the punk-friendly *Melody Maker* attacked the 'innumerable layers of gloss and veneer wrapped around a band doing little more than going through the motions'. The establishment press was no kinder, with *The Times* skewering the Earls Court show as 'one of those events that justify the emergence of the new wave bands: the triumph of technology over music'. Well-used to hostile British journalists, it's easy to imagine Queen swatting the criticism away. But unbeknownst to the media, the band had begun to take their own long hard look at those 'innumerable layers of gloss'.

## Queen's First EP (1977)

Personnel:
Freddie Mercury: piano, vocals
Brian May: guitars, vocals
Roger Taylor: drums, vocals
John Deacon: bass
Producers: Queen, Roy Thomas-Baker
Studios: Trident, London, August 1973; Wessex Sound, London, August 1975; Sarm East, London, September-November 1975; The Manor, Oxfordshire, July 1976
Release date: UK: 20 May 1977
Chart place: UK: 17
Running time: 12:79
Side One: 1. 'Good Old-Fashioned Lover Boy' (Mercury), 2. 'Death On Two Legs (Dedicated to...)' (Mercury)
Side Two: 1. 'Tenement Funster' (Taylor), 2. 'White Queen (As It Began)' (May)

On 20 May, EMI released new Queen product in the shape of this rather unimaginatively-titled four-track EP. It was a curious release, bundling together one recent song with three older cuts going back to 1974/1975. If the intention was to introduce new fans to earlier material, a question mark hung over why not all four Queen composers got a look-in – despite several fine contributions to the catalogue, John was overlooked. Packaged in an uninspiring sleeve, the EP reached only 17 in the UK, though its top-20 placing at least ensured that the opening cut later made it to the tracklist of the iconic 1981 *Greatest Hits* compilation (though not the US edition).

As *Queen's First E.P.* nosed into the British charts, Roger locked himself away in a studio with Mike Stone and produced a handful of solo tracks. Along with demos of 'Fight From The Inside' (a menacing rocker with a post-punk vibe) and 'Sheer Heart Attack' (a revamped version of a tune originally meant for the album of the same name, but which hadn't made the cut), Taylor came up with the rather derivative *Physical Graffiti*-era Led Zeppelin soundalike 'Turn On The TV'. This was two different songs pieced together, enlivened with a humorous intro featuring Roger trying out one of his falsetto screams before giving a chesty cough. The track became the B-side of the first solo Queen-member release. The A-side was 'I Wanna Testify' – a chunky, R&B-flavoured track with a title and chorus idea borrowed from a 1967 record by The Parliaments (who eventually became Parliament). It found Roger providing his distinctive brand of rhythm guitar and imitating a doo-wop vocal section. The song told the story of a man on the slide, drinking away his job and marriage while offering stern words of warning to anyone thinking of following him on his descent. Though sung with an appealing gruff irony, the track received little airplay, and stiffed in the charts; its trajectory wasn't helped by a cheap video which saw Roger barely able to contain a self-deprecatory smirk as he mimed to the recording. The record cost £5000 to produce, and Roger later brushed it off as simply 'a pleasant excursion' that he wasn't in any hurry to repeat.

### News of the World (1977)

Personnel:
John Deacon: bass
Brian May: guitar, vocals
Freddie Mercury: vocals, piano
Roger Taylor: drums, vocals
Producers: Queen, Mike Stone
Studio: Basing Street, London, July-September 1977; Wessex Sound, August 1977; Sarm East, London (Mixing), September 1977
Release dates: UK: 28 October 1977, US: 1 November 1977
Chart places: UK: 4, US: 3
Running time: 37:96
Side One: 1. 'We Will Rock You' (May), 2. 'We Are The Champions' (Mercury), 3. 'Sheer Heart Attack' (Taylor), 4. 'All Dead, All Dead' (May), 5. 'Spread Your Wings' (Deacon), 6. 'Fight From The Inside (Taylor)
Side Two: 1. 'Get Down, Make Love' (Mercury), 2. 'Sleeping On The Sidewalk' (May), 3. 'Who Needs You' (Deacon), 4. 'It's Late' (May), 5. 'My Melancholy Blues' (Mercury)

Co-produced by Queen and Mike Stone, the sixth album is the band's first reactive record. For all punk's blatant hostility, it had served as a wake-up call for the group, reminding them that elaborate production and exorbitant recording costs weren't essential to the making of exciting rock music. Prior to the August sessions, Brian and Roger made off-the-cuff remarks to the music press, suggesting a change was on the cards. 'They may have been overproduced', was Brian's verdict on *A Night at the Opera* and *A Day at the Races*, while Roger admitted that US sales of the last album had fallen short of expectations, and that some sort of a rethink might be in order.

Of course, there was no way Queen was ever going to make a punk record. Freddie still couldn't stand the Pistols or their champions in the music press, having been stung by a recent *NME* article that ran a front-page photo of him emblazoned with the headline, 'Is This Man A Prat?' For Mercury, the political slant of punk left him cold, and he famously insisted, 'I like to write songs for fun, for modern consumption. People can discard them like a used tissue afterwards'.

Though *News of the World* flirted with a bit of acidic social commentary, it encapsulated Freddie's vision by sounding like a record that had been thrown together for the sheer hell of it. A couple of songs were solo demos that the other band members added to. Apart from its two opening tracks, very little of the album was to achieve long-standing fame or acclaim. Yet precisely *because* it wasn't a lavish sequel to the previous two *Marx Brothers* records, it helped re-energise Queen's career.

The LP was recorded at Basing Street and Wessex Sound studios – the latter a converted church hall in North London, where – ironically – The Sex Pistols were embroiled in ongoing attempts to record their first album. Though the two bands largely made a respectful peace with each other (Brian and John 'Johnny Rotten' Lydon even managing to have a nice chat about music one afternoon), the Pistols' dissolute bassist Sid Vicious couldn't resist causing trouble. Staggering drunk into a Queen recording session one day, he sneered at Freddie and asked if he was still intent on 'bringing ballet to the masses'. Freddie had recently fed this quote to the media in response to questions about his Vaslav Nijinsky-inspired leotard. Later dismissed by Roger as a 'moron', Vicious (real name John Ritchie) was put in his place when Mercury – according to legend – called him 'Mr Ferocious', grabbed him by the scruff of the neck and ejected him from the studio.

Having already booked a November US tour, Queen imposed a two-month limit on recording their new opus. Clock-watching had never been their style, and the deadline forced them to come up with more-basic arrangements. This is none more evident than on the opening song 'We Will Rock You' – recorded using handclaps and foot stomps, with a brief guitar solo towards the end. The song's genesis went back to a spring concert at Stafford's New Bingley Hall, where Brian noticed the audience singing along fervently to many songs. Even after the band left the stage, the crowd continued, breaking into a rendition of Rodgers and Hammerstein's 'You'll Never Walk Alone' – a song Gerry and the Pacemakers popularised in the rock-'n'-roll era, and now religiously sung at football matches. Brian returned to the hotel, intent on creating a song based around a simple, memorable chant, with an arrangement a crowd of people without musical instruments could easily join in with.

In the end, 'We Will Rock You' was more than a mindless sing-along, with three verses packed with violent imagery that seemed to tap into the punk anger swirling around London in 1977. The lyric takes the form of a belligerent address to a mud-and-blood-spattered youth – possibly a Sid Vicious-like character – who aspires to be a 'big man someday' but, in the meantime, must submit to being put 'back into your place'. The chanted chorus is stern and foreboding, sounding less like the promise of a good time, and more like a threat.

The ever-inventive Mike Stone made a vital contribution to the recording by recruiting various studio staff (including the tea lady) to contribute handclaps and foot stomps. The latter were done on specially-created drum risers, and treated with a short electronic delay to make the crowd sound much louder. The result sounded thuggish, summoning the primal immediacy of early-1970s glam rock but without the party spirit. Brian's scratchy solo – which sounded both virtuosic *and* like the clumsy noodling of a punk let loose in a guitar shop – did little to ease the tension.

Though Freddie and Brian had often found themselves exploring radically different musical territory, they also enjoyed an uncanny symbiosis on more than one occasion. On *News of the World,* they came together as true musical brothers – Freddie's 'We Are The Champions' cutting perfectly into Brian's 'We Will Rock You'.

Speaking about 'We Are The Champions' to *Circus* magazine in 1978, Mercury admitted, 'I was thinking about football when I wrote it'. Imagining – as Brian had done – a song that would unite the audience and give them something to feel a part of, he came up with the ultimate stadium anthem and a lyric that hostile critics would inevitably misinterpret. In the piano-led verses, the song evokes the spirit of the

Sinatra pop standard 'My Way' – even making some specific references: 'Regrets, I've had a few' becomes 'Bad mistakes, I've made a few'. Exploding from a barrage of drums and guitars, the chorus appears to find Freddie trumpeting his triumph over all the critics and naysayers who've ever stood in his way. A more-sympathetic interpretation is that the 'We' is inclusive – inviting listeners to defiantly face up to adversity.

The album shifts up a gear with Roger's 'Sheer Heart Attack' – a song that had waited at least three years to get onto a Queen record. It's a willfully ugly morass of wild rhythm guitars, pummelling bass and flailing drums (the bass and most of the guitars played by Roger), with a sneering, stammering lyric that manages to evoke Johnny Rotten and 'My Generation'-era Roger Daltrey. The track is also reminiscent of the nihilistic roar of The Stooges, whose iconic albums *Raw Power* and *Fun House* predated and influenced British punk. But unlike The Stooges and their progeny, 'Sheer Heart Attack' boasts a sonic precision and musical style that is Queen down to its bones. Even Roger's choice of guitar (a rare 1967 Fender Esquire Broadcaster) is telling – a subtle hint to musos everywhere that this is no primitive racket played on scrapheap-scavenged instruments.

There aren't many songs in rock history inspired by the death of a pet cat, but Brian's 'All Dead, All Dead' is one of them. Featuring an exquisite piano part and an angelic Brian vocal (An earlier take had Freddie at the mic), the song has a fairy-tale quality not unlike earlier Brian numbers like 'White Queen (As it Began)'. Also like that song, there are touches of Shakespearean language and a creeping sense of English nostalgia. The cat in question had been a childhood pet of Brian's, but he masked the lyric's meaning in layers of ambiguity, leaving listeners wondering who exactly is 'all dead'.

The mellow mood continues with John's piano-based story song 'Spread Your Wings', which is Queen's only true Bruce Springsteen moment. It tells the story of a hotel-dwelling drifter called Sammy, who dreams of escaping from his dead-end job at 'The Emerald Bar'. In the verses, his boss sneers at him for daring to imagine a better life for himself, after which the majestic choruses urge him to 'fly away, far away'. The arrangement gets heavier as the song progresses, with dramatic power chords and a suitably airborne Brian solo. Sung majestically by Freddie, it's side one's third song to focus on the travails of a disaffected young person – a theme that chimed with the spirit of the times. John later confessed that Sammy was a fictional version of himself, and that the song expressed his anxiety about the possibility of one day having to return to a life of penury.

Side one ends with Roger's 'Fight From The Inside': another song shot through with punk disaffection. Roger provides his usual strident vocals and also plays bass – the result of the track being (like 'Sheer Heart Attack') an extension of his original demo. There are more crunching guitars – also played by Taylor – and a foreboding drum rhythm evoking jackboots stomping in darkened alleyways. The narrator is full of disdain for the person he's addressing, telling him he's a 'fool' and a 'money-spinner tool'. The target is a successful pop star whose image adorns countless teenage bedroom walls, while his self-righteous political pronouncements litter the airwaves.

Side two's opener – Freddie's 'Get Down, Make Love' – treads a dark path between erotic fantasy and feverish nightmare. The song is a milestone in Freddie's career and the moment when he gleefully begins to celebrate his sexuality. Though not a dance track, the vibe somehow evokes New York's gay-club scene, which Mercury had become steeped in. John's edgy bass riff plays a crucial role, while Roger's sudden snare drum tattoos ramp up the tension. But the most hair-raising part is the instrumental interlude, where a slow-pounding drum rhythm is layered with hellish vocal screams and unearthly sound effects. These unique sounds came not from a synth, but from the boffin-like antics of Brian, who'd fed his Red Special into Wessex Sound's Eventide harmonizer.

'The quickest song I ever wrote in my life' is how Brian once described 'Sleeping On The Sidewalk' – a blues song recorded quickly one afternoon at Wessex without Freddie's involvement. May later recalled that the three musicians played in the same room facing each other, with Roger providing a loose shuffle rhythm and John grooving away on his Fender Precision bass. May took the lead vocal, spinning a yarn about an impoverished young trumpet-player busker who is spotted by a major record executive, whisked off into a life of fame, then dropped back onto his street corner when his records stop selling. About as far away from the classic Queen sound as it's possible to get, this track is great fun but remains one of the band's least-known deep cuts.

Freddie and John's creative partnership had been flourishing for the previous couple of years, Mercury appreciating John's pop sensibility and knack for writing songs that were a little outside Queen's usual remit. Originally, 'Who Needs You' – Deacon's second offering on the album – had been tried (somewhat improbably) as a reggae track before finding its final feel as a Latin-tinged number. Freddie's delicate vocal inflections and emotive delivery are entirely in sync with the laid-back mood, and it sounds like a performance to which he devoted much tender loving care. Brian and John share acoustic guitar duties, the former also playing maraca before turning in a dazzling Spanish-style solo.

The album's big rock showstopper is Brian's 'It's Late'. Buried away as the penultimate track, it still manages to throw the surrounding songs into shadow. Brian later explained that the lyric was inspired by thinking about his former New Orleans sweetheart Peaches, and the resulting pangs of guilt he'd felt as a married man. Influenced by the structure of Greek tragedy, he created three distinct scenes – the protagonist is first at home with his wife, then with his illicit lover in a hotel room, then back at home with his wife again, now racked with remorse. Dominated by a distinctive lurching riff, the track gave Brian a chance to try out a new guitar technique called 'tapping' or 'hammering', which here involved attacking the fretboard with a sustained barrage of rapid-fire notes.

The album ends in the smoky late-night bar ambience of Freddie's 'My Melancholy Blues'. If 'Somebody To Love' caught him in Aretha Franklin mode, this song saw him paying tribute to his beloved Liza Minnelli and the movie *Cabaret*. The lyric draws from a deep well of jazz-flavoured sentimentality, conjuring the archetypal jilted lover alone at the piano long after the party has fizzled out. The song breaks with the Queen tradition of ending an album in a spirit of high drama, instead simply offering a brief fadeout.

Even today, *News of the World* is skewered by more long-term fans, while its admirers view it as a successful reboot of the Queen concept. Significant sections of the record seem to underachieve deliberately, and a bluesy looseness defies critics to aim the usual accusations of pompous art rock. With two songs apiece by Roger and John, the LP also represented the beginning of a shift in the group's power axis – the two underdogs flexing their muscles and grabbing a fuller share of the spotlight. In Roger's case, his two songs dragged Queen kicking and screaming into the late-1970s (and beyond), giving the band's music a new-wave edge entirely missing from the records of many of their competitors.

Even the album's physical presentation was a break from the past. The group had refused EMI's requests to show their faces on the previous two covers. For *News of the World*, they finally relented in their contrary way by becoming the first (and probably last) rock group in history to be depicted dead at the hands of a huge, bald, sad-looking robot. The painting was the creation of American illustrator Frank Kelly Freas, and was based on his 1953 image adorning an issue of *Astounding Science Fiction* magazine. Roger – along with Brian one of Queen's two sci-fi nerds – remembered the image from childhood and invited Freas to adapt it for the new album cover. Eerie and serene – despite its brutal theme – the finished painting shows the slain Freddie and Brian cradled in the robot's giant hand, while John and Roger's corpses flutter to the ground. All four wear the same outfits from the *A Day at the Races* gatefold – a tacit acknowledgement that Queen's mid-1970s art-rock incarnation is – to quote a line from Brian's song – 'all dead and gone'.

Along with the newspaper-referencing album title, the cover could be interpreted as Queen's ironic response to years of being savaged by the popular press. (It's surely no coincidence that it's only Freddie – the most maligned Queen member of all – who's pictured covered in blood). Brian has always maintained that the robot was supposed to be a benevolent creature, though this puts a puzzling spin on the inner gatefold's bonus scene of it menacing a terrified crowd.

The public's first introduction to Frank (the robot's nickname, bestowed in honour of his creator) had come three weeks earlier with his headshot adorning the 'We Are The Champions' single cover ('We Will Rock You' on the B-side). The single was a number-2 smash in the UK, reaching 4 in the US, helped by a memorable *in-performance* video shot in front of 900 fan-club members at New London Theatre in Drury Lane.

The album's fortunes were a mixture of triumph and disappointment. In the States, it reached number three: the group's highest-charting LP there to that point. But in the UK, it only reached 4, denying Queen a hat trick of chart-topping albums. It also sent out a clear signal that they could no longer hope to be top dog in a music scene turned upside down by punk and new wave. Tellingly, an album that *did* top the charts in November 1977 was the Sex Pistols' *Never Mind the Bollocks*.

Reviews for the Queen LP were mixed, with *The Washington Post* praising the record's 'intelligence and moderation', while *Record Mirror* described it as 'not a bad album... but it could have been better'. The musicians themselves seemed happy with their new direction – Brian telling *Circus* magazine: 'Our separate identities come to the fore on this album. Every cut is different from the one before it, and there's no concept at all'. Despite the undoubted chagrin of their art-rock-loving fans, Queen had decisively turned a creative corner and would never again record an album in the style of the *Marx Brothers* LPs.

In addition to the album release, 28 October was also notable for the taping of yet another BBC session. This sixth and final outing (broadcast on 14 November) was introduced by John Peel – the veteran British broadcaster who'd recently become a dyed-in-the-wool punk convert. In a nod to Peel's taste, the band delivered a no-frills selection of songs, including a fast, guitar-led 'We Will Rock You'. 'Spread Your Wings' was presented in a pared-down, faster arrangement with a heavy, extended coda.

The same month, Queen received a Britannia Award from the British Phonographic Industry, which had decided that 'Bohemian Rhapsody' was the best British single of the past 25 years. As usual, the group were too busy to bask in triumph, being already deep in rehearsal for the next bout of live work. They finished the year with a two-month US tour, opening the shows with the alternative version of 'We Will Rock You'. Keen to promote their new musical direction, they played at least half the material from *News of the World,* with Freddie singing Brian's 'Sleeping On The Sidewalk' and leading his comrades through an apocalyptic version of 'Sheer Heart Attack'. Roger took the plunge as lead vocalist in concert for the first time, performing an excerpt from 'I'm in Love With My Car'.

It was on this tour that a hallowed Queen tradition was birthed – Brian and Freddie perching on high stools to perform 'Love Of My Life'. Though reaction from American fans was muted, later performances in Europe and South America were to find vast crowds passionately singing along, sometimes so loudly that Freddie would stop and give them the floor.

For Brian, the tour was memorable for an emotional reconciliation with his father, Harold, who'd always struggled to accept his son's decision to pursue a music career at the expense of astronomy. Queen's achievements had so far done nothing to thaw relations between the pair – their disagreements casting a pall over Brian's attempts to enjoy his success. For the Madison Square Garden show on 1 December, Brian had both his parents flown in on the Concorde – a particular thrill for Harold, who'd helped design the aircraft's blind-landing system during his years with the Ministry of Aviation. Brian met up with his dad backstage after the show and was touched to discover that Harold had finally seen the light and was overcome by the crowd's evident love for his son's music. 'He told me, 'I get it, I understand now'', Brian revealed with tears in his eyes in a TV interview many years later – by which time Harold had passed away.

Though the critics still complained, Queen's latest US odyssey was yet more proof that they were now a major fixture on the American arena circuit. It was their first tour without any support acts to bolster ticket sales. Freddie told *Circus* magazine: 'There's so much happening on stage that I doubt there'd have been room for another band anyway. We have so much material we want to play for people now, that it would've been far too long a concert'.

Even while older, more-cynical admirers complained that the band had abandoned their art-rock roots, Queen were making new fans and holding their own against a generation of new bands and artists. But having survived the ground zero of 1977's punk, their search for continuing relevance and musical innovation wasn't about to become any easier.

# 1978 – Thunderclap by God

1978 saw yet another explosion of young musical talent, as the new wave sounds of The Police, Elvis Costello and Blondie gained traction in the British charts. Though Queen hadn't been around long compared to acts like The Who and Led Zeppelin, they were already being viewed as musical dinosaurs. *News of the World* had been a valiant attempt to get back to basics, but the band understood that they'd need continual change and evolution if they had any hope of staying competitive.

Though ostensibly on holiday for the first few weeks of 1978, they found time to conclude some ongoing business problems, ending their management contract with John Reid. He'd achieved great things for Queen, but the relationship had soured due to him inevitably splitting his time between them and his other star client Elton John. Brian later claimed that the fallout with Reid became so fractious, towards the end of 1977, that the group came close to breaking up. The divorce papers finally came through in February 1978; the documents chauffeur-driven to Roger's newly-acquired country home in Surrey, where the four band members were freezing their boots off in the back garden filming the promo clips for 'Spread Your Wings' and 'We Will Rock You'. Legend has it that the freezing musicians crammed themselves into the back of Freddie's Rolls Royce to sign the papers.

The band decided to form their own company – Queen Productions – reportedly paying each of them an annual salary of just over £500,000 and setting them on the road to becoming the UK's highest-paid company directors. Their lawyer Jim Beach left his top-paid job with law firm Harbottle & Lewis, and became Queen's official business manager, overseeing the new empire. Though Beach was being paid for his legal expertise, it was understood that Queen would be the captains of their own destiny from now on. John Deacon had already proven to be an astute financial operator. Since the end of the Trident era, he'd kept a beady eye on the band's business dealings and made sure that concert, recording and merchandise contracts brought in every possible penny. He now turned his attention to scrutinising the new income tax laws of Jim Callaghan's Labour government, which – much like the mid-1960s Harold Wilson administration – had a fondness for swallowing the profits of top-grossing rock bands. In Deacon's view, it would shortly become necessary for Queen to do what The Rolling Stones famously did in 1971: become tax exiles. Given how much of Queen's time was eaten up touring North America and Europe, this was doable. However, there was now the added twist that any new recording would have to occur outside the UK. For a band that had always made the south of England its geographical and spiritual home, this was a significant step.

The band's first 1978 release was the UK single 'Spread Your Wings' on 10 February. It was a song of sunny optimism and hope. But – in terms of Queen success – it crashed and burned, reaching only 34 in the charts. By then, the group was finishing rehearsals for another European tour which was due to begin in Stockholm on 12 April. The levitating Crown lighting rig was again an intrinsic part of the show's introduction – although, at one concert in Brussels, its grandeur was undercut when a chain hoist slipped during takeoff, and Brian was nearly squashed underneath. The malfunction proved serendipitous, with the crowd cheering as the performance restarted. In a 2012 Radio 1 interview, Brian recalled: 'When we eventually went back on, there was this great bond between us and the audience, as they'd realised we're human and stuff can go wrong. It was one of the greater nights that I remember'.

Further euphoria was in store at the Pavillion de Paris on 23 and 24 April – the two dates marking the first time Queen ever played in France. Their music had taken a long time to penetrate the French market, but 'We Are the Champions'/'We Will Rock You' had finally done the trick in 1977, topping the charts for six weeks and ensuring the band now received a heroes' welcome. 'Well, that's Paris ticked off', Freddie was heard to mutter as he came off stage, having witnessed the entire audience of 7000 on its feet from the opening bars of the first song to the closing moments of the encore.

As the tour came to an end, 'It's Late' began an inglorious chart trajectory as a US-only single, finally stalling at 74 and joining the previous 'Spread Your Wings' as Queen's second single to flop in 1978. The below-par performance of these two records alerted Queen to the necessity of another musical rethink. They were wondering if the next album needed to be braver and bolder if it was to compete with the exciting new wave music lighting up the airwaves in both the UK and the US. Rather than seek fresh input though, they elected to rehire the safe pair of hands that was Roy Thomas Baker. He'd recently been working with American new wave group The Cars, whose June-released debut album caught Queen's attention just as they were winding down from the tour. The record was a massive success – its lean, contoured sound striking a chord with legions of young music fans.

Queen felt that reuniting with Baker would help them recapture the personal chemistry and creative magic of their earlier peak years. Despite their continued professional triumph, the friendships within the band had begun to fray. It was now common practice for them to arrive at concerts in separate limos, only meeting briefly backstage before heading out to greet the adoring crowds.

The group's new tax-exile status was behind the decision to record in two European locations, spending no more than two months in each country, thus escaping tax bills in both. Recording commenced in mid-July at Mountain Studios in a casino complex in Montreux, Switzerland, before moving in September to Super Bear Studios in the hills above Nice, France. For the first time, they were making a record without the invaluable contribution of Mike Stone, whose summer work schedule couldn't accommodate ping-ponging between two foreign countries. In his place was sound engineer Geoff Workman and his assistant John Etchells – the latter a familiar face from Queen's first two BBC sessions recorded back in 1973 and 1974.

The sessions started in piecemeal fashion, with Deacon and Taylor arriving in Montreux on their own. Back in London, Freddie was helping with pre-production on the second album by his friend Peter Straker, whose debut Freddie had somehow found time to produce the previous spring. Meanwhile, Brian had just become a father for the second time – to a son called James – and was reluctant to depart too hastily. When he and Mercury finally joined the others at Mountain Studios, they were impressed with the cavernous recording space known as The Salon, with its banister-walkways and concealed spotlights. But in the end, the vast room was inconducive to the desired team spirit. Also, the control room was in the basement, which necessitated the rigging up of closed-circuit TV so the group could see Baker when he spoke to them. This was particularly important for Freddie, who liked to gauge from the producer's facial expression whether a vocal performance had hit the spot.

The sessions often found the band at loggerheads over song ideas and arrangements. Brian told Queen biographer Mark Blake in 2010: 'We were all getting into our own things, and nobody much liked what the other guys were doing'. While touring and playing live remained enjoyable, the arduous writing and recording process was increasingly feeling like a chore.

## Jazz (1978)

Personnel:

Freddie Mercury: vocals, piano

Brian May: guitars, vocals

Roger Taylor: percussion, vocals

John Deacon: bass

Producers: Queen, Roy Thomas Baker

Studios: Mountain Studios, Montreux, July-August 1978; Super Bear, Berre-les-Alpes, September-October 1978

Release dates: UK: 10 November 1978, US: 14 November 1978

Chart places: UK: 2, US: 6

Running time: 44:48

Side One: 1. 'Mustapha' (Mercury), 2. 'Fat Bottomed Girls' (May), 3. 'Jealousy' (Mercury), 4. 'Bicycle Race' (Mercury), 5. 'If You Can't Beat Them' (Deacon), 6. 'Let Me Entertain You' (Mercury)

Side Two: 1. 'Dead On Time' (May), 2. 'In Only Seven Days' (Deacon), 3. 'Dreamers Ball' (May), 4. 'Fun It' (Taylor), 5. 'Leaving Home Ain't Easy' (May), 6. 'Don't Stop Me Now' (Mercury), 7. 'More Of That Jazz' (Taylor)

Of all the 1970s Queen albums, *Jazz* is the most divisive – hailed by some as a dizzying smorgasbord of treats, it's dismissed by others as a badly-produced morass of creative dead-ends. The first thing to notice is the 13-song tracklist – the longest sequence since *Sheer Heart Attack,* which had also featured 13 tracks. However, this time there were no medleys or song fragments – each writer seemingly determined to have his contributions stand alone as finished statements.

The record is oddly sequenced and feels musically bumpy in a way that even *A Night at the Opera* did not. That record's stylistic tangents seemed possessed of their own curious inner logic. But on *Jazz,* the juxtapositions seem truly random. An oft-quoted example is Freddie's 'Let Me Entertain You' – an obvious curtain-raiser left to languish at the end of side one. And the album's most commercial cut – 'Don't Stop Me Now' – is buried second-to-last on side two.

Though *Jazz* contains some fine songwriting and arranging, several songs fall back too easily on Queen clichés. Their patented vocal arrangements *are* in evidence, but often sound rather clean and clinical. But perhaps a more serious accusation against the album is its curiously flat and compressed sound, with the guitars lacking their usual roar and the drums – for the first time – robbed of the Taylor thunder.

The collection kicks off with Freddie's 'Mustapha' – the most exotic Mercury tune for several years, and a throwback to the enigmatic writing style he'd employed on earlier albums. Beginning with an *a cappella* vocal sounding like a Muslim call for prayer, the song cleverly makes use of invented words and phrases with a distinctly Arabian flavour. The band creates a colourful and inventive arrangement that rocks hard but never detracts from the Middle East flavour. Given Freddie's newly-liberated lifestyle, it's perhaps surprising that he chose this moment to again celebrate his Persian roots, and in so explicit a way. That said, the song's intriguing web of fictitious phrases suggests that his tongue was in his cheek – a view confirmed by his later admission that the lyric was 'complete gibberish'.

It's difficult to imagine a more jarring contrast to 'Mustapha' than Brian's 'Fat Bottomed Girls' – a humorous paean to adolescent sex, which owes much of its flavour to the bump-and-grind of southern American bands like ZZ Top. Brian wrote the song on Freddie's prompting, after they'd enjoyed the sights and sounds of the annual Tour de France as it passed through Montreux in mid-July. Freddie's 'Bicycle Race' adopted a more literal approach to the subject matter, but Brian allowed his fevered imagination to take him off on a tangent with a lyric celebrating the physical anatomy of the female cyclists.

Freddie's piano ballad 'Jealousy' gave him a chance to display the sensitive side shown on songs like 'You Take My Breath Away' and 'My Melancholy Blues'. It's a solid ballad rather than a spectacular one, its chief attraction being the sitar-like sound of the old Hallfredh guitar Brian had used on 'White Queen (As It Began)'.

Freddie ups his game with 'Bicycle Race' – a head-spinning kaleidoscope that throws a nod to his previous dalliances with cod-opera and show tunes. The central vocal hook seemed designed to lodge in the brains of a whole generation of school kids – this being the late-1970s, many UK children still lived on their bikes. Though this song's inspiration had also been the Tour de France, the lyric is a tongue-in-cheek diatribe against products of modern culture (*Jaws*, *Star Wars* etc.) that lack the simple pleasures afforded by two wheels, a pair of pedals and a bell glittering in the summer sunshine. One of Freddie's most joyfully-inventive concoctions, 'Bicycle Race' even features an excerpt of jingling bells: bought from a variety of Montreux bicycle shops.

'If You Can't Beat Them' is the first of the album's two John Deacon songs – a straight-ahead power pop track with a section of heavily-phased guitars and a catchy chorus that – in a parallel universe – could've earmarked the track as a single. In fact, Deacon hadn't had a hit single since 'You're My Best Friend' two years before, but his writing was still showing an admirable consistency.

Side one ends with Freddie's 'Let Me Entertain You' – a frenetic rocker let down by brittle sonics. Despite its shortcomings, the track features some fiery bass-and-drums interplay, along with a mischievous lyric that finds Mercury promising his audience he'll show them some 'good merchandise'. There's a sense that the song was specifically tailored to pre-empt the band's endless parade of critics accusing them of peddling bad-taste, macho radio fodder.

Side two gets a turbocharged opening with Brian's fast rocker 'Dead On Time'. It joins 'Sweet Lady', 'White Man' and 'It's Late' in May's canon of metal deep cuts, though its frenetic pace (144 bpm) helps it to outshine many competitors. Brian later confessed he'd been proud of the song, and was disappointed when it was upstaged by 'Fat Bottomed Girls'. The track climaxes with an actual thunderclap, which Brian captured on a tape recorder one evening outside Super Bear. The album liner notes memorably credit this celestial sound effect with the phrase, 'Thunderbolt courtesy of God'.

John's 'In Only Seven Days' is another of his short-and-sweet pop songs in the 'Misfire'/'Who Needs You' tradition. But it's more cloying than either of those numbers, and has a slightly humdrum lyric detailing an uneventful holiday romance.

The sense of the band treading water continues into Brian's 'Dreamers Ball' – a sleepy jazz/blues number with acoustic guitars, brushes and an air of period nostalgia. May was inspired to write it after seeing a couple of performances at the high-profile Montreux Jazz Festival. In the context of Queen's supposed desire to tap into Baker's new-wave success with The Cars, the inclusion of 'Dreamers Ball' makes little sense until one remembers previous jazz-like Baker triumphs such as 'Good Company' and 'Bring Back That Leroy Brown'. 'Dreamers Ball' isn't a bad song by any means, having a well-crafted melody and an effortless sense of bohemian charm.

The album receives a shot-in-the-arm from Roger's 'Fun It'. Though he later dismissed it, it's a significant Queen song in the context of where their music was heading at the time. It was usually John and Freddie who flirted with black pop styles, but here Roger gets funky with a scratchy disco groove evoking the dance music then riding high in the charts. With vocals shared by Roger and Freddie, 'Fun It' is also significant for being the first Queen track to include electronic drums: a Pollard Syndrum Quad 478. This was an interlinked set of pads connected to a mini-console, capable of producing a range of analogue percussion effects. Used here to imitate the sound of tom-toms, its presence was further evidence that Queen were poised to reimagine their music as the 1980s hovered into view.

Brian's 'Leaving Home Ain't Easy' is yet another of his homages to homesickness. Like several other songs on *Jazz*, it seems to retread old ground without offering any new twists to the formula. The pleasant tune and husky May vocal ensure it's at least listenable. The most interesting production moment occurs during the break when the voice of the hero's pining wife is heard – interesting because this is Brian himself recorded at half-speed before the tape was then returned to normal speed.

Buried towards the end of the record, Freddie's piano-pumping 'Don't Stop Me Now' finds him calling himself 'a rocket ship on my way to Mars' and 'a sex machine ready to explode'. The arrangement features joyous call-and-response vocals and a scintillating guitar solo. But in later years, Roger revealed there was a darkness to the song which mirrored Freddie's dangerously overindulgent lifestyle at the time. The public at large remained blissfully unaware, of course, and 'Don't Stop Me Now' eventually became (to the surprise of Brian and Roger, who'd never rated it) an iconic, feel-good Queen anthem.

Though Freddie's beautiful singing over the 'Don't Stop Me Now' fade-out could've ended the album in great style, the record instead chugs to a close with Roger's 'More Of That Jazz'. The prowling drum rhythm is overlaid with jagged guitar riffs and Roger's bleary vocal, which occasionally rockets upwards into his trademark falsetto. The lyric appears to wallow in self-defeat and (alarmingly) disenchantment with rock-'n'-roll, which now only 'pays the bills'. Musically unremarkable, the song is notable for its edited montage of excerpts from 'Dead On Time', 'Bicycle Race', 'Mustapha', 'If You Can't Beat Them', 'Fun It' and 'Fat Bottomed Girls'.

*Jazz* found Queen standing at a creative crossroads – looking backwards but taking fumbling steps towards a musical future they hadn't quite grasped. Several songs demonstrated that they were still thinking big and angling for major chart success; others sounded jaded, or as if they'd been lost in translation between studio and finished recording. Significantly, for the first time since gaining full creative autonomy back in 1974, they'd failed to turn in a sonically-impressive record – a curious irony given this album was supposed to reignite some of that old Roy Thomas Baker magic.

A sense of anticlimax also hung over the cover design. It was inspired by the abstract, geometric images of Hungarian-French artist Victor Vasarely, by way of some graffiti Roger had spotted on the Berlin Wall back in April. The series of concentric circles was duly recreated, the title 'Jazz' emerging in bright pink lettering from the centre of the stark, monochrome image. The title also was Roger's – a 'good, short word ... with many meanings – not just music but 'jive", as he later told a Japanese interviewer. The inner gatefold featured a spectacular, wide-angle shot of the Salon at Mountain Studios – the band positioned yards apart from each other, surrounded by instruments and equipment. Along the bottom edge of the cover was a continuous line of fat-bottomed girls on bicycles, though it was only vinyl buyers who got the full-colour poster of 65 naked female models cycling around the track at Wimbledon Stadium. This curious event also provided footage for the 'Bicycle Race' promo video. That song and 'Fat Bottomed Girls' were released as a double-A-side single on 13 October, reaching 11 in the UK, despite some press accusations of sexism.

Controversy surrounded the $200,000 launch party for *Jazz*, which took place on 31 October in New Orleans, and featured strippers dressed as nuns, snake charmers, Zulu dancers, Caribbean steel bands, and all-female, naked mud wrestling. With Queen's critical stock already quite low, such spectacles weren't likely to garner a positive reaction. 'More of the same dull pastiche' was the verdict of *Rolling Stone's* Dave Marsh, who claimed that 'Fat Bottomed Girls' regarded women 'not as sex objects, but as objects, period'. *NME* was even more scathing, advising its readers, 'If you have deaf relatives, buy this low-class replica of Gilbert and Sullivan as a Christmas present'. Though chart action was quite strong (two in the UK and six in the US), the band found it hard to shake off the disappointment with their new work.

Ever suckers for punishment, the four frazzled musicians ended 1978 with a two-month US tour. This time they had an opulent new lighting rig, which was quickly named The Pizza Oven due to the phenomenal amount of heat it gave out. Another innovation was the introduction of a second, smaller stage, on which the band delivered intimate acoustic versions of 'Dreamers Ball, 'Love Of My Life' and ''39'. Not wishing to shake off his rock-'n'-roll credentials, Roger delivered a blazing tympani solo.

Despite the recent accusations of sexism, and prudish US record stores banning the naked poster from *Jazz*, Queen doubled down on the raunch-'n'-roll. For their Madison Square Garden shows, they recruited five New York club strippers to join them onstage (riding bicycles, naturally), and – spurred on by Mercury – continued to throw wild and excessive backstage parties.

The itinerary climaxed on 18 December after three performances at L.A.'s Inglewood Forum. Though the tour reviews were mixed, *LA Times* journalist Robert Hilburn allowed the band to bow out on a critical high, noting that their 'lavish musical textures provide some of the most consistently-appealing sounds in rock'. He also noted Freddie's new leather-sporting image, which made him resemble 'the lead in a campy Broadway-musical version of Marlon Brando's old film *The Wild One'*.

Having survived another year of madness, Queen had no intention of slowing down. They flew home for Christmas, their period of rest and rehabilitation as brief as ever. But their appetite for hard work knew no bounds and actually appeared to sustain them. Far from killing them off, the relentless touring was about to transform them into fully-fledged *live killers*.

# 1979 – So Much Fucking Noise

By 1979, the musical landscape of the UK (and, to a lesser extent, the US) had been transformed. Punk's shockwaves had subsided, and new-wave pop was flourishing. Disco – conveyer-belt dance music with roots in American club culture – was conquering the charts, much to the annoyance of many US rock fans. The dinosaurs rock bands were still lumbering on, though many lesser outfits were struggling or even going under. Prog rock was all but dead and buried, at least critically.

With healthy followings in Europe, Japan, Australia and North America, Queen weren't in danger of extinction. Their first 1979 release was the UK 'Don't Stop Me Now' single on 26 January. It was promoted with a video – the band miming beneath the Pizza Oven lighting rig. The promo highlighted how at least two band members had changed their image in recent times – Freddie sporting black leather, and John shaven-headed and looking rather like a primary-school teacher in a nondescript shirt and tank top. With its killer chorus hook, soul-revue-style backing vocals and singing guitar solo, the single was bound to do well. Sure enough, it rose to nine in the UK, and kept Queen visible in their homeland while they slogged around the continent.

It was a year of intermittent hard graft, with tours of Europe (17 January-1 March), Japan (13 April-6 May), Ireland/UK (20 November-22 December), a summer festival appearance in Germany and a Boxing Day charity concert in London. Even though there was some recording, 1979 was the first year since 1973 with no new Queen studio album. Brian later recalled that by this time, the stress of making records had become almost unbearable. In contrast, concert work was always straightforward, and it helped the group forget the creative difficulties that had dogged *Jazz*.

Freddie experienced some throat problems at the beginning of the European tour, but audience reaction was still through the roof. Given how tight and drilled the band was, it now finally seemed the right time to release a live album. Queen had long considered the idea – even right back to their historic Rainbow shows – but had never found the time or inspiration to make it a reality. Having put their recording career on hold, a live album seemed the best way to get product into stores before the decade was out. *Live Killers* became the final Queen long player of the 1970s.

## Live Killers (1979)

Personnel:

Freddie Mercury: vocals, piano

Brian May: guitars, vocals

Roger Taylor: percussion, vocals

John Deacon: bass

Producer: Queen

Recorded live on the Queen European Tour, January-March, 1979, using The Manor Mobile manned by Peter Greenslade, Ken Capper and Steve Cater

Release dates: UK: 22 June 1979, US: 26 June 1979

Chart places: UK: 3, US: 16

Running time: 86:05

Side One: 1. 'We Will Rock You (Fast)' (May), 2. 'Let Me Entertain You' (Mercury), 3. 'Death On Two Legs' (Mercury), 4. 'Killer Queen' (Mercury), 5. 'Bicycle Race' (Mercury), 6. 'I'm In Love With My Car' (Taylor), 7. 'Get Down, Make Love' (Mercury), 8. 'You're My Best Friend' (Deacon)

Side Two: 1. 'Now I'm Here' (May), 2. 'Dreamers Ball' (May), 3. 'Love Of My Life' (Mercury), 4. ''39' (May), 5. 'Keep Yourself Alive' (May)

Side Three: 1. 'Don't Stop Me Now' (Mercury), 2. 'Spread Your Wings' (Deacon), 3. 'Brighton Rock' (May)

Side Four: 1. 'Bohemian Rhapsody' (Mercury), 2. 'Tie Your Mother Down' (May), 3. 'Sheer Heart Attack' (Taylor), 4. 'We Will Rock You' (May), 5. 'We Are The Champions' (Mercury), 6. 'God Save The Queen' (trad. arr. May)

*Live Killers* was put together at Montreux's Mountain Studios in the spring of 1979. Though the band weren't impressed with the sound of *Jazz*, they'd felt at home at Mountain on the shores of Lake Geneva, so much so that they soon put in a successful bid to buy the facility outright. Resident engineer David Richards – who, after the purchase, ended up a full-time Queen employee – was given the task of ploughing through the European tapes to piece together a cohesive LP. The task was fraught with challenges, as many of the recordings were far from pristine quality. In later years, there was little agreement within the group about how 'live' some of the finished tracks actually were. Even if the performances weren't touched-up, it's now known that song segments from different shows were spliced together to banish inconvenient vocal errors and occasional bum notes.

The album's mixing was an uphill struggle, with no one ecstatic about the finished results. The band were uneasy with the inclusion of 'Bohemian Rhapsody', due to the use of backing tapes for the opera section. Though this worked fine in concert, in the context of a live record, it felt uncomfortably like cheating. '*Live Killers* wasn't my favourite album', Brian told *Pelo* magazine in 1981. By then, Roger had been criticising the record in public for two years. But despite the murky sound and ragged edges, the album had – and still has – its moments of late-1970s rock-'n'-roll glory.

The LP begins with the huge thunderclap Brian had recorded outside Super Bear. Then it's straight into the fast, heavy guitar version of 'We Will Rock You': a blistering onslaught that sets the bar high for the rest of the album. The double album's music is sprawling and diverse, and almost exactly divided between songs from the classic 1973-1976 art rock period and the subsequent punk-era years of 1977/1978. The performances are noisy and aggressive – the music angled at a young, late-1970s audience rather than the older listeners reared on the majesty of *Queen II*.

For any new fans coming to Queen in 1979, *Live Killers* was a treasure trove of discovery. It shone a light on the earliest material ('Keep Yourself Alive'), significant mid-1970s deep cuts ('Death On Two Legs', 'I'm In Love With My Car'), and steamrolling versions of some big time-honoured hits. 'Now I'm Here' and 'Brighton Rock' offered a glimpse into the band's long-standing fondness for stretching studio cuts into lengthy live epics. Meanwhile, their age-old trick of performing medleys (in this case, 'Death on Two Legs'/'Killer Queen'/'Bicycle Race'/I'm In Love With My Car') was preserved for posterity.

Finally, the record revealed to sceptical listeners that Queen music wasn't just a studio concoction but was the result of gutsy ensemble playing. Many years later, Roger told Queen biographer Mark Blake: 'I still find it extraordinary that the four of us could make so much fucking noise'. Taylor's drums were the bedrock of that noise of course – throughout the album, they're explosive, locking in with John's pile-driving bass. Though Brian had carved a reputation for orchestrated guitar parts, here, his Red Special snarls, roars and sings in real-time. He rarely leaves gaps unfilled, yet somehow his embellishments never seem gratuitous. As for Freddie, though his voice isn't always at its best, his ringmaster-like relationship with the audience is captured on the extended call-and-response section of 'Now I'm Here'.

*Live Killers* enjoyed a visually distinctive presentation. The front cover showed the band wreathed in smoke beneath the sweltering red, green and yellow lights of the Pizza Oven, at the climax of a Japanese show. (As a side note, the figure of Brian holding his Red Special aloft was superimposed into Koh Hasebe's photo.) The back cover showed Freddie cavorting in his new Village People-style attire, complete with peaked leather cap, and the inside gatefold was a collage of concert images taken across the years. Fans were treated to intriguing juxtapositions of the new, crew-cut-sporting John with his 1974 self, long-flowing mane present and correct. Roger's penchant for Rod Stewart-style tiger-skin trousers was proudly highlighted.

Perhaps the finest aspect of the whole package were the four matching red/green labels on the records themselves, each of which featured a different band member. For the first time since the debut LP, sleeve notes were provided, offering useful snippets of musical and technical information ('top fax and info' as Roger might have said in 1973) that wouldn't have been widely known at the time.

Not by any stretch of the imagination a *classic* live album, *Live Killers* is better than its reputation suggests. It even picked up a couple of favourable notices, with *Record Mirror* instructing its readers to 'bring out the champagne and the roses – this is a triumph'. If nothing else, the double LP captured the sun setting on Queen's balls-to-the-wall, hard-rock incarnation – their raw sound still geared towards indoor arenas, as opposed to the sports stadia that would become their home in the subsequent decade. By the time Queen released their next live album (*Live Magic* (1986)), they'd morphed into a sunny, high-energy, daytime-radio band; still able to rock, but more focussed on sing-along choruses and anthemic pop hooks.

Now that they were the official owners of Mountain Studios – and having no immediate plans to start a new album – Queen were happy to rent the facility out to other acts. Still tax exiles in early-summer 1979, they couldn't return to the UK in the wake of their latest Japanese excursion. Instead, they diverted to Musicland – the legendary east-Munich basement studio that Italian disco producer Giorgio Moroder had installed beneath the colossal high-rise Arabella hotel and residential block. The original idea was just to store their equipment while making enquiries about available engineers. Then they met Reinhold Mack, and the plan changed.

Mack was Musicland's resident genius engineer and sometime producer, whose vast technical skills had enhanced Moroder's disco recordings along with classic albums by Led Zeppelin, The Rolling Stones, and Mack's main star clients, ELO. He'd also produced Brian's hero Rory Gallagher. Queen's collaboration with Mack almost immediately resulted in a brand-new song being recorded: 'Crazy Little Thing Called Love'. 'I wrote it in the bath', Freddie told *Melody Maker* two years later, remembering how it popped into his head at Munich's Hilton hotel. It was a rockabilly pastiche in the Elvis tradition, written dripping wet using the handful of guitar chords Freddie knew. The recording came together so quickly that Freddie delivered a final take without even realising that Mack was rolling the tape. The track featured Mercury on Presley-style vocals and acoustic guitar, though Brian later overdubbed an electric solo. He disapproved of the track's retro simplicity, but Mack made things worse by insisting that Brian temporarily ditch his Red Special and Vox AC30 in favour of Roger's 1967 Fender Esquire (as previously used on 'Sheer Heart Attack') and a Mesa Boogie amp – to capture the authentic flavour of 1950s rock-'n'-roll. Brian admitted to *On the Record* in 1982: 'I kicked against it, but I saw it was the right way to go'.

'They were set in their ways, like pensioners', Mack later told Mark Blake, recalling how Queen appeared to him on first acquaintance. And it was Brian who gave him the most trouble. While Mack was a fast decision-maker, Brian worked at an agonising snail's pace. He and Mack also had major technical disagreements, not the least over how best to capture the complex harmonics of the Red Special. But as sessions advanced, Brian joined the others in recognising that Mack had brought something unique to their sonic palette and – more importantly – to their overall recording approach.

Firstly, there was his trademark chiselled sound – rooted in mid-1970s dance music and foregrounding meaty bass frequencies and huge, crunchy drums. Then there was his determination to break Queen's age-old habit of repeatedly recording backing tracks until they got the perfect take. Instead, Mack spliced takes together, editing out mistakes and creating the illusion of a flawless performance. Brian later told *On the Record*: 'We laughed, and said, 'Don't be silly, you can't do that'. But, in fact, you can. What you gain is the freshness, because often, a lot of the backing tracks are first-time through'.

Mack's energy and speed were infectious, giving Queen the kick in the pants that Roy Thomas Baker hadn't been able to provide the previous autumn. With myriad song ideas now flying around Musicland's claustrophobic confines, more finished tracks started rolling off the tapes. 'Coming Soon' – a Roger *Jazz* outtake – was given a dusting down, and quickly shaped up as a grooving, new-wave rocker with a mischievous lyric and a barbed-wire guitar solo. It was the second Taylor composition (after 'Sheer Heart Attack') to mainly be sung by Freddie, with Roger on chorus vocals. In fact, Mercury-sung Taylor songs were soon to become the norm, as the drummer's long-thwarted desire to notch up a hit single reached new heights.

Brian, too, was approaching the end of his long run as a regularly-featured lead vocalist. His 'Sail Away Sweet Sister' would be his final hurrah for many years, though even then, Freddie took the bridge. The windswept ballad – which featured beautiful Mercury piano and the sound of crashing waves – depicted a heartbroken man bidding his sister farewell as she prepares to abandon him for lands unknown. Brian later explained the song's mysterious dedication 'To the sister I never had', admitting he'd spent much of his adult life with a lingering sadness about being an only child.

There was more May heartbreak on offer with 'Save Me' – this one sung by Freddie and proffering a huge, impassioned chorus that would guarantee hit-single status the following year. Though the lyric detailing the plight of a forsaken lover sounded painfully personal, Brian later revealed that it had been inspired by the circumstances of a close friend. The song's recording marked a huge sea change in Queen's studio work by finally introducing a synthesizer into their sound world. The machine in question – a polyphonic Oberheim belonging to Roger – was used here to accompany the guitar solo. Though Taylor had previously used the Pollard Syndrum for novel percussion effects on *Jazz,* its inclusion wasn't too conspicuous. The Oberheim was more significant and broke Queen's unwritten (and quite often written!) *no-synths* rule. It was a telling sign that the band was poised on the cusp of a new era: ready, in fact, to greet the 1980s.

As the group pieced their new songs together with Mack that summer, the live version of 'Love Of My Life' from *Live Killers* was released as a UK single but crawled no higher than 63. It was their worst-performing British 45 since 'Keep Yourself Alive', though given it was a live rendition of a four-year-old song, the single's failure didn't cause too many sleepless nights.

Determined not to sink back into the album-tour-album rigmarole, Queen left Munich towards the end of July. They were thrilled with their new partnership with Mack, but had no desire to start slogging away at another LP. Nor were they in any immediate rush to get back to heavy touring. In August, they headlined the Saarbrücken Festival in Germany – Roger sheepishly sporting luminous green hair, after an accident with a Peroxide bottle. They found themselves going on stage after Rory Gallagher, but not before Brian cornered the genial maestro and acknowledged his artistic debt to him.

The late summer and early autumn found the band enjoying their first honest-to-God holiday since the pressures of fame and success had descended. Freddie and Roger kicked back as Wimbledon tennis punters, while John again savoured the delights of fatherhood, with the birth of his third child Laura.

Freddie was also limbering up for an entirely different experience: becoming a fully-fledged ballet dancer. The offer had come through from The Royal Ballet Company, which on Sunday, 7 October was staging a charity gala event at London's Coliseum Theatre. Wanting to recruit a cameo performer from outside the rarefied dance world, they initially approached Kate Bush, who turned down the offer. Freddie was a natural shoo-in and was a great success when the show was unveiled before ballet connoisseurs. Freddie had trained with company dancer Derek Deane, who later revealed that his student pushed himself so hard that he nearly did himself an injury. 'I thought it was brave and absolutely hilarious', Roger later told Mark Blake, having attended the performance and been tickled by the sight of his friend ('this silver *thing*') being gracefully tossed around the stage to an orchestral version of 'Bohemian Rhapsody'. Freddie also performed a version of 'Crazy Little Thing Called Love', hitting all the notes while executing dazzling dance moves. He told John Blake from the *London Evening News*: 'I did this wonderful leap. It brought the house down, and then they all caught me and I just carried on singing!' As the culmination of a decade in which he'd already become a world-famous singer and songwriter, this balletic display proved beyond all doubt that Freddie Mercury was no typical rock star.

October saw the release of the next Queen single. 'Crazy Little Thing Called Love' was publicised with a hammy video showing the group sporting black leather and shorter-than-usual haircuts (even Brian!), in the company of a male-and-female dance troupe. As the nation's pop lovers looked on in wonderment, a Brylcreemed Freddie posed on a gleaming motorbike, and paraded down a catwalk doing a hilarious stylized Elvis impersonation. In his black leather jacket and white t-shirt, he looked more like Arthur 'Fonzie' Fonzarelli from the American TV show *Happy Days*. A shades-wearing Brian exuded effortless cool when miming the Fender guitar solo he'd recorded through gritted teeth at Musicland.

The song and video were both radical departures for Queen, finally shining a spotlight on the mischievous sense of fun that had so often fuelled their musical experiments. The recording's period charm – as expertly realised by Mack – tapped into the same vein of 1950s nostalgia that had propelled the movie *Grease* to international acclaim the previous year. In 1979, the single also managed to be ahead of the curve, with retro rockabilly acts like Stray Cats waiting in the wings (Their first single was released nearly one year later). But perhaps the biggest accolade the single earned was that it was reportedly the record that reignited John Lennon's interest in contemporary pop music. Within a few months of its release, he came out of retirement and recorded his own homage to 1950s rock-'n'-roll': '(Just Like) Starting Over'.

As Queen rehearsed for their end-of-year UK tour, the single began its triumphant rise through the British charts, finally settling at number two. It was the third time in as many years that a Freddie song had stalled just shy of number one. But given how painlessly this one had been created, no one was complaining.

With the song having captured a new, younger audience, John and Roger made a memorable guest appearance on the live Saturday morning kids TV show *Tiswas* in November. Dodging the custard pies that were traditionally hurled at the show's guests, Roger also managed to explain the thinking behind their imminent UK tour: 'On the last British tour, we did very big places, like Stafford Bingley Hall and Wembley Arena. This time we thought we'd play in all the outer and smaller places, where you can get more atmosphere and it's not like playing a big mausoleum'.

The aptly named Crazy Tour kicked off in Ireland on 20 November, and ran for one month. As Roger had hinted, the itinerary included medium-sized venues, such as Liverpool's Empire Theatre, Bristol Hippodrome, and at least one former ice-skating rink (Tiffany's in Croydon). Most exciting of all, for Queen fans of a certain vintage, was a 14 December show at London's Rainbow Theatre.

After having flogged their way through every vast, impersonal arena in America over the past two years, the UK dates offered a warm and fuzzy nostalgia. Of course, that didn't mean a slump in the hard work – due to high ticket demand, they were obliged to play two shows across consecutive nights in some towns. There were also technical headaches, with some venues being too small to accommodate the Pizza Oven. Others could only do so after holes were drilled into the ceilings, at the band's expense.

When it came to the London Lyceum, Paul McCartney offered to help pay for the alterations, so he could have his lighting rig installed for the Wings show the following week. (Coincidentally, just a few nights before in Liverpool, Freddie and Brian played an impromptu version of Wings' recent hit 'Mull Of Kintyre'.) The stress and strife were all too much for long-term road manager Gerry Stickells, who suffered a nervous collapse mid-tour. Queen were seeing out the decade by pushing everything to the max, as usual.

The tour climaxed at Alexandra Palace on 22 December – Freddie marking the occasion by donning a silver lurex suit and throwing bananas into the audience. That night, video footage was captured of the band playing the next scheduled single, 'Save Me', with a view to it forming the basis of a promo video in the new year. Even then, the excitement wasn't quite over, for on Boxing Day, the group was again on stage at the personal invitation of Mr. McCartney. The occasion was the first in a series of charity concerts at the Hammersmith Odeon – organised by Paul to raise money for the then-war-torn Cambodia. Other acts booked for *Concerts for The People of Kampuchea*, between 26 and 29 December, included The Clash, Elvis Costello, The Pretenders and The Who, with Queen opening the run and Wings closing it. (*Their* performance on the final evening would be their last.)

While the second, third and fourth nights all contained multi-act bills climaxing with a headliner, the first night consisted of Queen alone. The band played a long, energetic set with much audience participation and onstage bonhomie, including Freddie emerging for the encore perched on the shoulders of a roadie dressed as Superman. The show was notable for featuring the final live performances of 'Don't Stop Me Now' (which was still several decades away from achieving its status as a Queen classic) and the destined-to-be-not-quite-so-loved 'Let Me Entertain You'. The show also hinted at future developments, with Brian's solo turn containing an excerpt from a floaty new composition that would eventually be titled 'In The Space Capsule' and used in the band's 1980 soundtrack to the movie *Flash Gordon*.

The show was the perfect end to a decade that had seen Queen rise from obscurity, adversity and penury, to become global stars, celebrated songwriters, and millionaires. Right to the very end, the naysayers carped, with *Sounds*' Crazy Tour review referring to Queen as a 'bunch of shrink-wrapped unit shifters'. But now that the band had a worldwide following, these critically-despised 'unit-shifters' were – and would continue to be – immune to the slings and arrows of press hostility. That's not to say they'd carried their entire audience with them intact. But by the end of the 1970s, any deserting fans had already been replaced by younger listeners who cherished 'We Are the Champions' and 'Don't Stop Me Now' far more than 'Brighton Rock' or 'The Prophet's Song'.

Through all of the decade's fashion changes, Queen had thrived. Cleaving together at all costs, maintaining a professional partnership long after the halcyon days of early friendship had faded, the band had conquered the 1970s. And though they'd never again be that group of ambitious young men who walked into Trident Studios in 1973, their personal relationships were destined to recover. By the end of the 1980s, the band would be as close as brothers once again. But a lot had to happen first.

As for the 1970s, one final triumph was in store. In the States, Elektra had baulked at releasing 'Crazy Little Thing Called Love' as a single but quickly changed their minds when American DJs got behind it. Needing no further prompting, the record roared up the charts, and by Christmas, had lodged itself at number one. It was the first time that any Queen record had ever occupied a top spot in the US. In several 1970s interviews, the band had spoken wistfully about the prospect of finally being number one in America. It was the grail coveted by every major rock band since The Beatles. Yet despite Queen's incredible success, that grail had so far eluded them. It's remarkable to think that where the magisterial, decade-defining 'Bohemian Rhapsody' had fallen short, the frivolous 'Crazy Little Thing Called Love' had effortlessly succeeded. Catchy and tuneful, and with huge crossover appeal, Queen's most retro record was, ironically, a clear signpost to their glittering future.

# Postscript: The Show Did Go On

When Queen stepped onstage at *Live Aid* on Saturday, 13 July 1985, a reported two billion viewers worldwide caught their breath. Here was a band who'd reached their commercial peak several years before: an act that had become part of the scenery and been largely taken for granted, even by their fans. But there was something in the way Freddie Mercury strode onto that stage at Wembley Stadium that signalled the arrival of a pivotal moment for him, his band and everyone watching.

While other groups and artists had happily entertained the punters, Freddie had the air of a man who was about to own them body and soul. For the next 20 minutes, a casually dressed Brian May, Roger Taylor and John Deacon laid down a pulverising backing, while their old friend and comrade majestically sang his way through a selection of their best-known numbers. Hitting every note despite suffering from a sore throat, he preened and strutted for the cameras, brandishing the *Freddie stick* that had been his stage prop for the last 15 years. Four of the six songs played dated back to the far-off days of the 1970s.

More than any other act at *Live Aid,* Queen seemed to understand that they were there to act as a human jukebox. Armed with none of the lights or smoke bombs they'd once used to blind and deafen their audiences, they still proved a dazzling spectacle. The four members' musical symbiosis was undeniable, even to the most strenuous Queen naysayer.

Yet somehow, the lion's share of the triumph belonged to Freddie. His onstage persona – honed and polished through years of concerts – had become truly larger than life. Since 1970, he'd morphed his way through various physical incarnations – donning and discarding kimonos, leotards and black leathers in his search for this final, ultimate avatar: the white-t-shirted, blue jeans-wearing global superstar with the cropped hair and bristling moustache. Despite all his 1970s achievements, and despite even the world-famous 'Bohemian Rhapsody' video in which the shaven-headed, moustached Freddie was nowhere to be seen – it was his Live Aid self that was destined to become the one that everybody (and that's pretty much *everybody*) remembered. A mere six and a half years after that big day, he was gone.

Ending a Queen book at the end of 1979 inevitably feels a little frustrating. The band's 1980s career was *another* dazzling spectacle, at least in some parts of the world. But the decade also brought problems for the band. Though their partnership with Reinhold Mack at Musicland produced a chart-topping US album (*The Game*) in 1980, the Munich sessions saw further fragmentation of the band's long-tested friendships. Freddie partied harder than ever, and toyed with the idea of a solo career – his first and only solo album *Mr. Bad Guy* becoming a mid-decade, UK top-10 hit. 'Easy' Deacon announced that he no longer wanted Brian to play guitar on his songs (which didn't come to pass), and annoyed Roger by joining Freddie in insisting that Queen record more disco music in the style of John's Chic-inspired 'Another One Bites The Dust' – Queen's biggest-ever single, and one that briefly won them a whole new urban/black audience in the US. The resulting album – 1982's *Hot Space* – was admired by critics but largely hated by fans: a curious inversion of the dynamic that had persisted throughout the 1970s. That album also featured the number one UK single 'Under Pressure' – their first and only collaboration with their old hero/nemesis David Bowie. Yet again, it was a track built on an epochal Deacon bass line.

As Freddie dialled up his gay image and lifestyle, and the group's music drifted further away from hard rock, Queen's star began to fall in the US. The final nail in the coffin was the video for Deacon's 1984 song 'I Want To Break Free' (from the Mack-produced album *The Works*), which showed the band posing as British soap characters, dolled-up in drag. The joke went unappreciated by American fans, and resulted in falling ticket and record sales there until Freddie one day announced he couldn't be bothered playing concerts in the US anymore. It was a damp-squib climax to the band's American dream, especially considering the phenomenal amount of hard graft they'd put in on the arena circuit throughout the 1970s. *C'est la vie, darlings.*

With North America fading, Queen turned their attention to other markets. In 1984 – during a cultural boycott of that country's apartheid – Queen outraged the international community by agreeing to play a series of concerts at South Africa's Sun City venue. On a happier note, they captured a vast new audience in South America – their triumph encapsulated by two headline shows at the 1985 Rock in Rio festival before an estimated audience of 500,000. Meanwhile, steady as a rock, Japan continued to love their Queen.

Back in the UK, they carved up the charts with four huge hit singles from the number-1 album *The Works* – the most iconic of which – 'Radio Ga Ga' – was written by Roger Taylor. His moment of glory had been a long time coming, and he followed that success in 1986 with his 'A Kind Of Magic' from the album of the same name. That record (which flopped in the States) was at least partly a soundtrack to the film *Highlander*: the first Queen movie work since *Flash Gordon* in 1980. With Mack as producer, the record rocked hard in places and offered up one undoubted Queen classic in Brian's atmospheric 'Who Wants To Live Forever'. But like all Queen's 1980s LPs, *A Kind of Magic* also contained some less-than-convincing slivers of paper-thin pop.

With *Live Aid* giving Queen a career boost in 1985, they embarked on their mammoth Magic Tour in Europe, which climaxed with two 1986 Wembley Stadium shows – the second of which became legendary when released on video as *Queen Live at Wembley*. There was then a triumphant Knebworth performance that turned out to be Freddie's last live hurrah.

Solo projects then ensued, with Roger fronting a new outfit called The Cross and Brian producing records for artists as diverse as Bad News (a fictional comedy metal combo containing The Young Ones' Adrian Edmondson, Nigel Planer and Rik Mayall) and soap actress Anita Dobson (Brian's new flame following his divorce from Chrissie). With typical aplomb, Freddie teamed up with the classical opera singer Montserrat Caballé and released the *Barcelona* album, which reached the UK top 30. John picked up plenty of high-profile session work with the likes of Elton John and Errol Brown. John also appeared wearing a green wig in the video for comedy pop outfit Morris Minor and the Majors' 'Stutter Rap (No Sleep Til Bedtime)'.

With reports of Mercury's mysterious ill health spreading across the media, Queen managed to record two more albums – 1989's *The Miracle* and 1991's *Innuendo* – before the terrible truth emerged that Freddie had been diagnosed with AIDS. By the time the world properly understood just how unwell Freddie was, he'd passed away, leaving the three remaining Queen members to later stage a huge charity show in his honour, and patch together a posthumous album of outtakes called *Made in Heaven* (1995). Freddie left behind him a hole that could never be filled, though Brian and Roger have valiantly tried many times to do so.

The story of Queen's post-Freddie afterlife could fill another book, but it's safe to say that it covers a period when Queen ceased being a mere *band*, and became a global *brand*. There's been a computer game, a West End stage musical, a cinema biopic, countless CD and vinyl reissues and compilations, and major tours in which Brian and Roger utilised the unlikely company of such singers as Paul Rodgers (formerly of Free and Bad Company) and Adam Lambert (an *American Idol* runner-up), billing themselves not quite as Queen, but as Queen +.

Again, critics have carped and fans have cheered in great abundance. Even the North Americans have jumped back on board. Fans struggling to get behind a Freddie-less Queen have also grumpily noted the non-involvement of John Deacon. Long retired from the music business, he now leads a very quiet life indeed. He even gave the Deacy Amp to his old mate Brian as a parting gift.

For all of Queen's later trials and triumphs, their 1973-1979 period still exerts a magnetic hold over many fans and admirers. The music they recorded in that hallowed decade now seems to offer a glimpse into a different world – a hugely mysterious and beguiling one. Starting with 'Keep Yourself Alive' and finishing with 'Crazy Little Thing Called Love', Queen's 1970s laid the groundwork for everything they were to do and be in the future. It was an era when musicians with the wackiest ideas could be left alone by major record companies to construct the grandest of conceits. They were times of rich imagination, dizzying ambition, and quite obscene quantities of vocal overdubs. Most importantly, it was the decade when Freddie Bulsara turned his extraordinary vision of a regal rock band into reality through the sheer power of his own will – first convincing his fellow musicians of the idea, then joining forces with them to sell it to an audience of millions.

'We'll never get away with it, Fred', the tall physics graduate told his bucktoothed graphic designer friend upon first hearing how Smile were to become Queen, in the early days of 1970.

'Nonsense darling, they'll love it', his friend replied.

And they did.

# A Brief Guide to Compilations and Live Albums

## Compilations

Queen have been well-served with compilations, both when they were still a working four-piece *and* after Freddie's death. What follows is a quick and by-no-means-complete guide to the main collections, which include (either heavily or exclusively) material recorded and/or released in the 1970s. For reasons of space, not all releases are listed, nor several vinyl and CD box sets which have compiled Queen's entire discography in a variety of tempting (and usually expensive) packages. For more detailed information on releases covered or not covered here, please delve into Georg Purvis' stupendous Queen compendium *Complete Works* (see bibliography).

### Greatest Hits (EMI/Elektra, 1981)
Chart places: UK: 1, US: 14
The original, 17-track hits album was released in the UK in 1981 following the huge international success of *The Game* album and subsequent *Flash Gordon* soundtrack. The British version collected many (though not all) of the group's beloved 1970s singles and four early-1980s hits. (One of those – 'Save Me' – was recorded in 1979.) The 1970s-released songs were: 'Bohemian Rhapsody', 'Killer Queen', 'Fat Bottomed Girls', 'Bicycle Race', 'You're My Best Friend', 'Don't Stop Me Now', 'Crazy Little Thing Called Love', 'Somebody To Love', 'Now I'm Here', 'Good Old-Fashioned Lover Boy', 'Seven Seas Of Rhye', 'We Are The Champions' and 'We Will Rock You'.

Outside the UK, the tracklist varied depending on which singles had been hits in the relevant countries. The original 14-track US version omitted the UK-only single 'Save Me', 'Don't Stop Me Now' (a US flop) and 'Good Old-Fashioned Lover Boy' (released only in the UK), but added 'Keep Yourself Alive' despite that also having flopped in the US. The American version was re-released in 1992 as a sort-of companion piece to *Classic Queen* (see below), with yet more tracklist tinkering and the bizarre inclusion of songs that hadn't even been US singles.

### Classic Queen (Hollywood, 1992)
Chart place: US: 4
Released the year after Freddie's death, this collection is popularly viewed as the US equivalent to 1992's *Greatest Hits II*. Though Queen's

US career nosedived in the late-1980s, the inclusion of 'Bohemian Rhapsody' in the 1992 comedy movie *Wayne's World* saw America re-embrace Queen, capturing a new generation of fans. The tracklist is broader in scope than the 1980s-exclusive *Greatest Hits II*, thanks to the inclusion of 'Bohemian Rhapsody', 'Stone Cold Crazy', 'Tie Your Mother Down' and 'Keep Yourself Alive'.

## Queen Rocks (Parlophone/Hollywood, 1997)
Chart place: UK: 7
This collection was designed to highlight the band's heavier side. It contained a mixture of singles and deep cuts, with the 1970s represented by 'We Will Rock You', 'Tie Your Mother Down', 'Seven Seas Of Rhye', 'Stone Cold Crazy', 'Now I'm Here', 'Fat Bottomed Girls', 'Keep Yourself Alive', 'Sheer Heart Attack', 'I'm In Love With My Car' and 'It's Late'. Eagle-eyed readers will spot the paucity of Freddie songs, which seems unfair given his undoubted talent for writing heavy rockers. Brian, on the other hand, came out well, with Roger scoring silver. Never a heavy rocker, John's songs were entirely absent.

## Stone Cold Classics (Hollywood, 2006)
Chart place: US: 45
A 12-song compilation put together as a companion to a Queen-devoted episode of American TV series *American Idol*. Over half the songs were from the 1970s – namely 'Stone Cold Crazy', 'Tie Your Mother Down', 'Fat Bottomed Girls', 'Crazy Little Thing Called Love', 'We Will Rock You', 'We Are The Champions' and 'Bohemian Rhapsody'.

## The A–Z of Queen, Volume 1 (Hollywood, 2007)
No chart placings
Released just one year after *Stone Cold Classics*, this 11-track, alphabetically sequenced compilation was exclusively available from Amazon.com and Wal-Mart, and featured a second disc of promo videos and live performances (though there's barely anything here to tempt fans of 1970s Queen). On the audio disc, the 1970s material comprised 'Bohemian Rhapsody', 'Bicycle Race', 'Crazy Little Thing Called Love', 'Don't Stop Me Now', 'Fat Bottomed Girls' and 'Good Old-Fashioned Lover Boy'.

## Absolute Greatest (Parlophone/Hollywood, 2009)

Chart places: UK: 3, US: 195

Available in many different formats – including a vinyl box set and a
2-CD edition accompanied by a lavish 52-page book – this 20-track
compilation includes the following nine 1970s hit singles: 'We Will Rock
You', 'We Are The Champions', 'Crazy Little Thing Called Love', 'You're
My Best Friend', 'Don't Stop Me Now', 'Killer Queen', 'Seven Seas Of
Rhye', 'Somebody To Love' and 'Bohemian Rhapsody'. All songs were
remastered from the original tapes, and there was a tasty bonus disc
of live performances: many from the 1970s. The live tracks comprised
'White Queen (As it Began)' (Rainbow Theatre, 1974), 'Killer Queen' and
'You Take My Breath Away' (Earl's Court, 1977), 'The Millionaire Waltz'
and 'My Melancholy Blues' (The Summit, 1977), 'Dreamers Ball' (Pavilion
de Paris, 1979), 'We Will Rock You (fast)' and 'Let Me Entertain You'
(Nippon Budokan, 1979), 'I'm In Love With My Car' and 'Now I'm Here'
(Hammersmith Odeon, 1979).

**Deep Cuts, Volume 1** (1973-1976) (Island, 2011)
Chart place: UK: 92
**Deep Cuts, Volume 2** (1977-1982) (Island, 2011)
Chart place: UK: 175

The three *Deep Cuts* releases (the third focussed exclusively on the
post-1970s) were – as the title implied – an attempt to anthologise
notable album tracks, fan favourites and the odd flop single. As such,
these collections are the best way (excluding streaming!) for Queen
newcomers to sample the lesser-known material without forking out
for the original albums. *Volume 1* includes: 'Ogre Battle', 'Stone Cold
Crazy', 'My Fairy King', 'I'm In Love With My Car', 'Keep Yourself Alive',
'Long Away', 'The Millionaire Waltz', "39', 'Tenement Funster', 'Flick Of
The Wrist', 'Lily Of The Valley', 'Good Company', 'The March Of The
Black Queen' and 'In The Lap Of The Gods… Revisited'. In addition to
a smattering of early-1980s cuts, *Volume 2* includes 'Mustapha', 'Sheer
Heart Attack', 'Spread Your Wings', 'Sleeping On The Sidewalk', 'It's Late',
'Dead On Time', 'Sail Away Sweet Sister' and 'Jealousy'.

**Queen Forever** (Virgin EMI/Hollywood, 2014)
Chart places: UK: 5, US: 38

Though intriguingly billed as featuring songs the band had 'forgotten
about', this US compilation has a slight whiff of *cash-in* about it. The
overall concept was to highlight Queen's softer, more-ballad-friendly

side. The selection of 1970s material is standard on the single disc version, though it's nice to find 'Drowse', 'Dear Friends', 'Long Away' and 'Nevermore' on the 36-track, double-disc *Deluxe Edition*.

# Live Albums

Though *Live Killers* remains the most iconic recording of the 1970s Queen in action, it does have a small number of stablemates. Below is a brief summary of these releases, only two of which are true live (i.e., 'in-concert') albums.

**Live at the Beeb** (Band of Joy, 1989)
Chart place: UK: 67
Released in Freddie's lifetime, this album collected the tracks recorded for the first and third *Sounds of the Seventies* BBC radio sessions – broadcast on 5 February and 3 December 1973. The songs are as follows: 'My Fairy King', 'Keep Yourself Alive', 'Doing All Right', 'Liar' (from the first session), and 'Ogre Battle', 'Great King Rat', 'Modern Times Rock 'N Roll' and 'Son And Daughter' (from the third). Despite the music's undoubted historical significance, and the beautiful black-and-white photo adorning the jacket, the record barely troubled the charts. However, this didn't stop Hollywood Records from later issuing their own version in the States and Canada: titled *At the BBC* (1995).

**Live at The Rainbow '74** (Virgin EMI/Hollywood, 2014)
Chart places: UK: 11, US: 66
Another of the many releases to be made available in multiple tempting editions (with tracklists too copious and diverse to list here), the basic single-disc version of *Live at The Rainbow '74* gave fans the chance to experience (or re-experience) the legendary two-night stand at The Rainbow on 19 and 20 November 1974. Those able and willing to shell out for the double-CD/quadruple-vinyl set also got the earlier Rainbow show, from 31 March 1974. This concert is historically interesting in that it was originally planned as Queen's third album, only shunted into the sidings thanks to Brian's health crisis on the band's first US tour. By this time, they'd written and released *Sheer Heart Attack*, and had stirred several of their newer songs into the set. As a result, the multi-disc *Live at The Rainbow '74* releases provided a fascinating amalgamation of *Queen II* darkness and *Sheer Heart Attack* wackiness, with some hard-rocking moments from the debut thrown in for good measure. The DVD edition of the November performances included some footage (three songs plus a Brian guitar solo) from the earlier March show.

**A Night at The Odeon – Hammersmith 1975** (Virgin EMI/
Hollywood, 2015)
Chart places: UK: 40, US: 40

This release documents the significant Christmas 1975 show which was
broadcast live on BBC TV's *The Old Grey Whistle Test*. It was later widely
bootlegged after being aired (in edited form) on Radio 1 in February
1976. Though Freddie and Brian were stricken with the flu on the night,
it's still a tight and dynamic performance, opening (unusually) with 'Now
I'm Here', and uniquely featuring 'Seven Seas Of Rhye' as an encore
(because they forgot to play it earlier in the evening!). Issued as a single-
CD and double-LP – along with the inevitable DVD/Blu-Ray for those
with deeper pockets – the set contains key early tracks from the first
three albums and some genuine curios such as 'Bring Back That Leroy
Brown' and 'See What A Fool I've Been'. Along with the perennial live
favourite 'Big Spender', there's also a rock-'n'-roll medley consisting of
snatches of 'Jailhouse Rock', 'Stupid Cupid' and 'Be-Bop-A-Lula'.

**On Air** (Virgin EMI/Hollywood, 2016)

Rather more satisfying than the earlier *Live at the Beeb* collection, this
elegant package finally collected all six of the *Sounds of the Seventies*
BBC Radio sessions from 1973-1977. Being 2016, there were of course,
multiple versions (2-disc CD, 6-disc deluxe CD and 3-LP vinyl). Along
with the eight selections from *Live at the Beeb*, the tracklist included 'See
What A Fool I've Been', 'Keep Yourself Alive', 'Liar', 'Son And Daughter'
(Session 2, 1973), 'Modern Times Rock 'N Roll', 'Nevermore', 'White
Queen (As It Began)' (Session 4, 1974), 'Now I'm Here', 'Stone Cold
Crazy', 'Flick Of The Wrist', 'Tenement Funster' (Session 5, 1974), 'We Will
Rock You', 'We Will Rock You (fast)', 'Spread Your Wings', 'It's Late' and
'My Melancholy Blues' (Session 6, 1977).

# Resources

## Books
Blake, M., *Is This the Real Life? -The Untold Story of Queen* (Aurum, 2011)
Blake, M., *Magnifico! – The A to Z of Queen* (Nine Eight, 2021)
Clerc, B., *Queen – All the Songs* (Black Dog & Leventhal, 2020)
Doherty, H., *The Treasures of Queen* (Carlton, 2019)
Hodkinson, M., *Queen – The Early Years* (Omnibus Press, 2004)
Jones, L., *Bohemian Rhapsody – The Definitive Biography of Freddie Mercury* (Hodder, 2012)
May, B., *Queen in 3-D* (The London Stereoscopic Company, 2017)
Purvis, G., *Queen – Complete Works: Revised and Updated* (Titan, 2018)
Rider, S., *Queen – These are the Days of Our Lives: The Essential Queen Biography* (Kingsfleet, 1993)
Sheffield, N., *Life on Two Legs: Set the Record Straight* (Trident, 2013)
White, R., *Queen in Cornwall* (Antenna, 2011)

## Selected Articles and Press Interviews
Several quotes in this book are taken from press interviews and articles presented in extracted form in other works, where the publication and author credits are not always given and/or where the precise issue numbers and dates of publication are omitted. Below is a list of the articles I consulted, though some of these were online, and titles were not always provided.

Davis, A., 'Queen Before Queen', *Record Collector* (November 1995-January 1996)
Cohen, M., 'Queen: The New British Invasion', *Phonograph Record* (March 1976)
Doherty, H., 'The Year Queen Lizzy Shook America: Queen and Thin Lizzy Tour the USA', *Melody Maker* (1977)
Horide, R., 'Queen Deserves Rock's Royal Crown, *Circus* (19 January 1978)
Ross, R., 'Queen's Four-Fold Strategy for Global Conquest', *Circus Raves* (March 1975)
Strick, W., 'Queen's Old Tale of Success', *Circus* (31 January 1977)
Tiven, J., 'Queen Swings Both Ways', *Circus* (August 1976)
Turner, S., 'Queen: Four Queens Beat Opera Flush' *Rolling Stone* (November 1976)

## Websites

brianmay.com
queenlive.ca
queenarchives.com

## On Track series

Alan Parsons Project – Steve Swift 978-1-78952-154-2

Tori Amos – Lisa Torem 978-1-78952-142-9

Asia – Peter Braidis 978-1-78952-099-6

Badfinger – Robert Day-Webb 978-1-878952-176-4

Barclay James Harvest – Keith and Monica Domone 978-1-78952-067-5

The Beatles – Andrew Wild 978-1-78952-009-5

The Beatles Solo 1969-1980 – Andrew Wild 978-1-78952-030-9

Blue Oyster Cult – Jacob Holm-Lupo 978-1-78952-007-1

Blur – Matt Bishop – 978-178952-164-1

Marc Bolan and T.Rex – Peter Gallagher 978-1-78952-124-5

Kate Bush – Bill Thomas 978-1-78952-097-2

Camel – Hamish Kuzminski 978-1-78952-040-8

Caravan – Andy Boot 978-1-78952-127-6

Cardiacs – Eric Benac 978-1-78952-131-3

Eric Clapton Solo – Andrew Wild 978-1-78952-141-2

The Clash – Nick Assirati 978-1-78952-077-4

Crosby, Stills and Nash – Andrew Wild 978-1-78952-039-2

The Damned – Morgan Brown 978-1-78952-136-8

Deep Purple and Rainbow 1968-79 – Steve Pilkington 978-1-78952-002-6

Dire Straits – Andrew Wild 978-1-78952-044-6

The Doors – Tony Thompson 978-1-78952-137-5

Dream Theater – Jordan Blum 978-1-78952-050-7

Electric Light Orchestra – Barry Delve 978-1-78952-152-8

Elvis Costello and The Attractions – Georg Purvis 978-1-78952-129-0

Emerson Lake and Palmer – Mike Goode 978-1-78952-000-2

Fairport Convention – Kevan Furbank 978-1-78952-051-4

Peter Gabriel – Graeme Scarfe 978-1-78952-138-2

Genesis – Stuart MacFarlane 978-1-78952-005-7

Gentle Giant – Gary Steel 978-1-78952-058-3

Gong – Kevan Furbank 978-1-78952-082-8

Hall and Oates – Ian Abrahams 978-1-78952-167-2

Hawkwind – Duncan Harris 978-1-78952-052-1

Peter Hammill – Richard Rees Jones 978-1-78952-163-4

Roy Harper – Opher Goodwin 978-1-78952-130-6

Jimi Hendrix – Emma Stott 978-1-78952-175-7

The Hollies – Andrew Darlington 978-1-78952-159-7

Iron Maiden – Steve Pilkington 978-1-78952-061-3

Jefferson Airplane – Richard Butterworth 978-1-78952-143-6

Jethro Tull – Jordan Blum 978-1-78952-016-3

Elton John in the 1970s – Peter Kearns 978-1-78952-034-7

The Incredible String Band – Tim Moon 978-1-78952-107-8

Iron Maiden – Steve Pilkington 978-1-78952-061-3

Judas Priest – John Tucker 978-1-78952-018-7

Kansas – Kevin Cummings 978-1-78952-057-6

The Kinks – Martin Hutchinson 978-1-78952-172-6

Korn – Matt Karpe 978-1-78952-153-5

Led Zeppelin – Steve Pilkington 978-1-78952-151-1

Level 42 – Matt Philips 978-1-78952-102-3

Little Feat – 978-1-78952-168-9

Aimee Mann – Jez Rowden 978-1-78952-036-1

Joni Mitchell – Peter Kearns 978-1-78952-081-1

The Moody Blues – Geoffrey Feakes 978-1-78952-042-2

Motorhead – Duncan Harris 978-1-78952-173-3

Mike Oldfield – Ryan Yard 978-1-78952-060-6

Opeth – Jordan Blum 978-1-78-952-166-5

Tom Petty – Richard James 978-1-78952-128-3

Porcupine Tree – Nick Holmes 978-1-78952-144-3

Queen – Andrew Wild 978-1-78952-003-3

Radiohead – William Allen 978-1-78952-149-8

Renaissance – David Detmer 978-1-78952-062-0

The Rolling Stones 1963-80 – Steve Pilkington 978-1-78952-017-0

The Smiths and Morrissey – Tommy Gunnarsson 978-1-78952-140-5

Status Quo the Frantic Four Years – Richard James 978-1-78952-160-3

Steely Dan – Jez Rowden 978-1-78952-043-9

Steve Hackett – Geoffrey Feakes 978-1-78952-098-9

Thin Lizzy – Graeme Stroud 978-1-78952-064-4

Toto – Jacob Holm-Lupo 978-1-78952-019-4

U2 – Eoghan Lyng 978-1-78952-078-1

UFO – Richard James 978-1-78952-073-6

The Who – Geoffrey Feakes 978-1-78952-076-7

Roy Wood and the Move – James R Turner 978-1-78952-008-8

Van Der Graaf Generator – Dan Coffey 978-1-78952-031-6

Yes – Stephen Lambe 978-1-78952-001-9

Frank Zappa 1966 to 1979 – Eric Benac 978-1-78952-033-0

Warren Zevon – Peter Gallagher 978-1-78952-170-2

10CC – Peter Kearns 978-1-78952-054-5

Also available from Sonicbond

## Decades Series

The Bee Gees in the 1960s – Andrew Môn Hughes et al 978-1-78952-148-1

The Bee Gees in the 1970s – Andrew Môn Hughes et al 978-1-78952-179-5

Black Sabbath in the 1970s – Chris Sutton 978-1-78952-171-9

Britpop – Peter Richard Adams and Matt Pooler 978-1-78952-169-6

Alice Cooper in the 1970s – Chris Sutton 978-1-78952-104-7

Curved Air in the 1970s – Laura Shenton 978-1-78952-069-9

Bob Dylan in the 1980s – Don Klees 978-1-78952-157-3

Fleetwood Mac in the 1970s – Andrew Wild 978-1-78952-105-4

Focus in the 1970s – Stephen Lambe 978-1-78952-079-8

Free and Bad Company in the 1970s – John Van der Kiste 978-1-78952-178-8

Genesis in the 1970s – Bill Thomas 978178952-146-7

George Harrison in the 1970s – Eoghan Lyng 978-1-78952-174-0

Marillion in the 1980s – Nathaniel Webb 978-1-78952-065-1

Mott the Hoople and Ian Hunter in the 1970s – John Van der Kiste
978-1-78-952-162-7

Pink Floyd In The 1970s – Georg Purvis 978-1-78952-072-9

Tangerine Dream in the 1970s – Stephen Palmer 978-1-78952-161-0

The Sweet in the 1970s – Darren Johnson from Gary Cosby collection
978-1-78952-139-9

Uriah Heep in the 1970s – Steve Pilkington 978-1-78952-103-0

Yes in the 1980s – Stephen Lambe with David Watkinson 978-1-78952-125-2

## On Screen series

Carry On… – Stephen Lambe 978-1-78952-004-0

David Cronenberg – Patrick Chapman 978-1-78952-071-2

Doctor Who: The David Tennant Years – Jamie Hailstone 978-1-78952-066-8

James Bond – Andrew Wild – 978-1-78952-010-1

Monty Python – Steve Pilkington 978-1-78952-047-7

Seinfeld Seasons 1 to 5 – Stephen Lambe 978-1-78952-012-5

## Other Books

1967: A Year In Psychedelic Rock – Kevan Furbank 978-1-78952-155-9

1970: A Year In Rock – John Van der Kiste 978-1-78952-147-4

1973: The Golden Year of Progressive Rock 978-1-78952-165-8

Babysitting A Band On The Rocks – G.D. Praetorius 978-1-78952-106-1

Eric Clapton Sessions – Andrew Wild 978-1-78952-177-1

Derek Taylor: For Your Radioactive Children – Andrew Darlington
978-1-78952-038-5

The Golden Road: The Recording History of The Grateful Dead – John Kilbride
978-1-78952-156-6

Iggy and The Stooges On Stage 1967-1974 – Per Nilsen 978-1-78952-101-6

Jon Anderson and the Warriors – the road to Yes – David Watkinson 978-1-78952-059-0

Nu Metal: A Definitive Guide – Matt Karpe 978-1-78952-063-7

Tommy Bolin: In and Out of Deep Purple – Laura Shenton 978-1-78952-070-5

Maximum Darkness – Deke Leonard 978-1-78952-048-4

Maybe I Should've Stayed In Bed – Deke Leonard 978-1-78952-053-8

The Twang Dynasty – Deke Leonard 978-1-78952-049-1

***and many more to come!***

# Would you like to write for Sonicbond Publishing?

At Sonicbond Publishing, we are always on the lookout for authors, particularly for our two main series. At the moment, we only accept books on music-related subjects.

On Track. Mixing fact with in-depth analysis, the On Track series examines the work of a particular musical artist or group. All genres are considered, from easy listening and jazz to 60s soul to 90s pop, via rock and metal.

Decades. An in-depth look at an important calendar decade in the career of a well-known artist or group.

While professional writing experience would, of course, be an advantage, the most important qualification is to have real enthusiasm and knowledge of your subject. First-time authors are welcomed, but the ability to write well in English is essential.

Sonicbond Publishing has distribution throughout Europe, North America and Australia and all books will also published in E-book form. Authors will be paid a royalty based on sales.

Further details are available from www.sonicbondpublishing.co.uk.

To get in touch, complete the contact form there or email info@sonicbondpublishing.co.uk

**Follow us on social media:**
Twitter: https://twitter.com/SonicbondP
Instagram: https://www.instagram.com/sonicbondpublishing_/
Facebook: https://www.facebook.com/SonicbondPublishing/

Linktree QR code:

# Queen - *on track*
## every album, every song

Queen on track
every album, every song
Andrew Wild
Paperback
144 pages
32 colour photographs
978-1-78952-003-3
£14.99
$21.95

**Every album by these
giants of rock.**

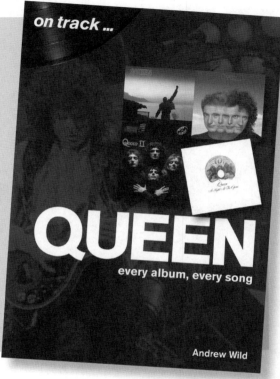

Everyone knows Queen and their most famous songs. 'Crazy Little Thing Called Love', 'Another One Bites the Dust', 'Under Pressure' and 'Bohemian Rhapsody' were huge hits wherever anyone could hear a radio. However, many contemporary reviews were savage, and yet their songs—from the radio-friendly hit singles to the early prog rock epics, from the cod-heavy bombast to the jazz pastiches, from the introspective ballads to the thumping anthems—continue to be heard all around the world.

This book examines Queen's music, album by album, track by track, in detail. Where possible, recourse to the original multi-track master tapes

has provided extra insight. Those familiar hits are revisited, but the classic album cuts - like 'Liar', 'March of the Black Queen', 'Death on Two Legs', and 'Dragon Attack', are given equal precedence. The book also examines the changes that these same four musicians went through – from heavy and pomp rock to pop as the chart hits began to flow – with a keen and unbiased eye.

Whether as a fan your preference is for the albums A Night at the Opera, Jazz or Innuendo, this detailed and definitive guide will tell you all you need to know. Queen had strength in depth. These are the songs on which a legend was built.